Student Book

Blueprint

4

B1 Intermediate

Peggy Anderson · Thomas Hong

Contents

Grammar and Structures	Listening / Reading	Writing / Speaking
Lesson 1 Present continuous with present and future reference	R & L: Discussing weekend plans with a friend	S: Future plans
Lesson 2 Simple present vs. present continuous	R & L: Preparing for a dinner party	W: An event planner for a get-together
Lesson 3 Action verbs and stative verbs	L: Self-introductions	S: Eating preferences
Lesson 4 Expressing preferences with *would rather*	R & L: Explaining a game's rules	W & S: Self-introductions, hobbies, and future plans
Lesson 5 Expressing preferences and making comparisons with prefer and *as... as*	R & L: Deciding what to watch on TV	S: Favorite TV shows, movies, and books
	L: TV genres	W & S: Personal preferences
	R & L: Comparing books and media	W & S: Opinions on living alone
	L: Problems living together	
	R: A magazine article about living on your own	
Lesson 1 Future tense	R & L: Visiting family	S: Your family
Lesson 2 Making predictions and expressing probability with *will* and *be going to*	R: An email about a family get-together	W: A family trip
	R: Online advice column	W: Ideas for a blind date
	R: Dating advice	S: Dating advice
Lesson 3 Modals of possibility	R & L: Going to the movie theater	S: Movie preferences
Lesson 4 *that* clauses	R & L: A night out	W & S: Predictions about the future
Lesson 5 Suggesting activities	R & L: A day trip	W & S: Fun things to do in your city or hometown
	R: A magazine article about the districts of Berlin	W & S: An advertisement for a new business
	R & L: Plans for next year	S: Plans for a weekend trip, including daily schedules
Lesson 1 Gerunds and infinitives	R & L: Olympic sports	S: Athletic dreams
Lesson 2 Suggestions and advice with gerunds, infinitives, modals, and *that* clauses	R & L: Planning to watch a sporting event	W & S: Favorite athletes and favorite sports to watch
	R & L: Fitness goals	S: Being punctual
Lesson 3 Future continuous tense	R & L: Fitness tips	S: Watching a sports event together
Lesson 4 Empty *it* and *that* clauses	R & L: Sports injuries	W & S: A fitness plan
	R: A friend's email about extracurricular activities	S: Eating habits
Lesson 5 Intensifiers		W & S: Health and fitness questionnaire
		S: Sports and other types of injuries
		W: An email to a friend
		W & S: Fitness routines and plans for reaching fitness goals
Lesson 1 Present perfect tense	R & L: Making a doctor's appointment	S: A time when you were sick
Lesson 2 Present perfect vs. simple past	R & L: Talking about your illness and symptoms	S: "I have never told a lie" game
Lesson 3 *too* and *enough*; *want / would like* + object + infinitive	R & L: At the dentist's	W & S: Role-play: A visit to the doctor
	R & L: Discussing problems with a therapist	W & S: How to treat an illness
	R: Analyzing your dreams	W: Pet allergies
Lesson 4 Past continuous tense; *when* clauses	R & L: Getting a prescription	S: Role-play: A visit to the therapist
Lesson 5 Modals of obligation	L: A doctor's call	S: "I have never ever" game
		W & S: Describing pictures

* Also, see the glossary in the back of the Workbook.

Contents

v

MODULE 1 When the Day Is Done

Module 1 Goals

Have short conversations with friends, and ask and answer simple questions about familiar topics (for example, hobbies, sports, and music)
Describe plans, arrangements, and alternatives
Understand discussions about daily life and be able to request assistance when needed
Discuss different things to do, places to go, etc.
Start, maintain, and close simple face-to-face conversations on topics that are familiar or of personal interest
Know enough vocabulary to talk about hobbies and interests, work, travel, news, and current events
Understand the main points in short newspaper and magazine articles about current and familiar topics

Preview

Look at pages 8 to 33. What pages are these things on?

a band playing live   _____

a nature show with a lion   _____

a creepy girl   _____

a crystal ball   _____

Discuss

Talk about the questions with a partner.

1. Which of your friends are good cooks?

2. What are some hobbies that you can do alone?

3. What hobbies can you only do with other people?

4. Where are some fun places to go in your city?

5. What do you like to do on rainy days?

Write

Choose one of the questions from above. Write a couple of sentences to answer it.

_____

_____

_____

Unit 1

Scan the QR code to watch a preview video.

Unit 2

| Lesson 1 | What are you up to tonight? |

A Model Conversation

Read the conversation. Then listen. `Track 02`

Nancy: Hey, how's it going, Ted?

Ted: I'm doing all right. How are you?

Nancy: I'm great. What are you up to tonight? Do you have any plans?

Ted: Well, I plan to stay in tonight. Why?

Nancy: Charlie's band is playing at the jazz club at 8:00. My friends and I are planning to watch them. Then we're going to a dance club. Would you like to join in?

Ted: That sounds like a lot of fun, but I'm sorry, I can't go out tonight.

Nancy: Really? How come?

Ted: My brother's in town for the weekend, and we're having a get-together with some friends. Tonight, we're cooking grilled salmon and watching football.

Nancy: Okay. I understand. Maybe we can go out Sunday. You can invite your brother.

Ted: Sure. Thanks!

B Vocabulary

Fill in the blanks with the correct words from the boxes to complete the summary.

football	grilled salmon	jazz	club	band

plans	staying in	get-together	join in	invite

Ted has **a** _____ tonight. He's **b** _____ with his brother and watching
c _____. They are having a **d** _____ with some friends, and they are cooking
e _____. Nancy and her friends want to go out. They will go to a **f** _____ club
to watch Charlie's **g** _____ play. Then they will go to a dance **h** _____. Nancy
asks Ted if he would like to **i** _____, but he can't. So Nancy asks Ted to go out on Sunday
instead, and she tells him he can **j** _____ his brother.

C In Your World

Ask a partner "What are you up to…" questions. Write his or her responses. Then tell the class.

- …tonight?

  _____

- …this weekend?

  _____

- …this summer?

  _____

Grammar

Present continuous with present and future reference

present continuous: subject + *be* + verb-*ing*		
statement	negative	question
They **are playing**.	They **are not / aren't playing**.	**Are** they **playing**?
about the present		about the future	
The present continuous is usually about actions happening right now. Time expressions such as (*right*) *now* or *at the moment* can be used.		The present continuous can also be used for definite future plans. Future time expressions such as *tonight* can be used.	
She**'s talking** on the phone (now). We**'re watching** football (at the moment).		I**'m staying** in (tonight). The band **is playing** at the jazz club (on Thursday).	

Grammar Practice

Put the words in order to make sentences.

1. are / what / doing / on / Saturday / you

   _____?

2. tonight / are / planning / to / football / watch / you / the / game

   _____?

3. right / jazz song / is / playing / the / now / band / a

   _____.

4. tomorrow / is / cooking / dinner / who

   _____?

5. my / I / get-together / and / roommate / planning / weekend / a / this / are

   _____.

Use the Language

Event planner

With a partner, choose and plan a special event such as a dinner party, watching a sports event on TV, or just a get-together for fun. Discuss all the details, including a place, a date and starting time, activities, food, and people to invite. When you are done, report the details of your event to the class.

Type of event	____ Dinner party	____ Sports event	____ Other get-together
Date and time			
Place			
People to invite			
Food			
Activities			

Dinner with Friends

Brief note

The phrases "help yourself" and "dig in" are often used at the start of a meal.
Help yourself. = Please take some (food).
Dig in. = You're welcome to start eating.

A Model Conversation

Read the conversation. Then listen.  Track 03

Ian: Debbie? Can I set the table?

Debbie: Yeah. But don't take out the turkey. Let's wait for Carla to get here.

Ian: But I'm starving! Why is she always late?

Debbie: Because she's working hard on a research project.

Ian: You're right. Sorry. I didn't mean to whine. Oh, good—here she is!

Carla: Hi, guys! Sorry I'm late. Wow! Everything smells so delicious!

Debbie: We made your favorite dish, too—vegetable pasta.

Carla: Yum! It looks tasty. Did you prepare all of this?

Debbie: Ian cooked all day!

Carla: Really? Well, everything looks fantastic! Thank you so much.

Ian: It was no problem. Help yourself, and dig in!

B Vocabulary

Fill in the blanks with the correct words from the box. Change the form if necessary.

set the table	take out	wait	starving	delicious
favorite	vegetable	tasty	prepare	turkey

1. I'm cooking. What's your _____ dish?

2. The _____ looks great! Who _____ it?

3. Are tomatoes a fruit or a _____?

4. Could you please _____? Dinner's ready.

5. A: Can we eat soon? I'm _____.

   B: Just _____. The food will be done soon.

6. Thank you for the _____ meal. Everything was so _____.

7. Don't _____ the pizza! It's not done yet.

C In Your World

Tell a partner your answers to the following questions.

- What's your favorite food?
- How often do you eat it?
- Can you prepare it?
- Why do you like it?

Then listen to your partner's answers. Share your partner's answers with the class.

Grammar

Simple present vs. present continuous

Temporary means for a certain period of time; not forever.

simple present vs. present continuous				
simple present		**present continuous**		
routine actions	He **runs** every day. I **practice** the piano on weekends.	actions now	He**'s running** right now. I**'m practicing** the piano now.	
general facts	Students **study**. She **lives** in Canada.	temporary facts	I**'m studying** biology this year. She**'s living** in a dorm.	
		future plans	We**'re going** out tonight.	

Grammar Practice

Fill in the blanks with the correct form of the verb in parentheses (simple present or present continuous). Then circle the correct usage.

1. I'm _____ (stay in) tonight.
   a. routine action   b. general fact   c. action now   d. temporary fact   e. future plan

2. Chickens sometimes _____ (eat) corn.
   a. routine action   b. general fact   c. action now   d. temporary fact   e. future plan

3. Over one hundred people _____ (come) to my coworker's wedding next week.
   a. routine action   b. general fact   c. action now   d. temporary fact   e. future plan

4. I always _____ (sleep) late on Saturday mornings.
   a. routine action   b. general fact   c. action now   d. temporary fact   e. future plan

5. I can't hear you. My father _____ (watch) basketball on TV, and it's very loud!
   a. routine action   b. general fact   c. action now   d. temporary fact   e. future plan

6. Sophia _____ (work) at a café for a few months, but in the fall she'll go back to school.
   a. routine action   b. general fact   c. action now   d. temporary fact   e. future plan

Listen to Speak

Listen to Marissa introduce herself. Put a check mark (✓) next to the details that are true. Track 04

1. Marissa is studying music. _____
2. She lives in an apartment. _____
3. She has a job. _____
4. She is eating dinner right now. _____

Now describe yourself to a partner. Include the following information:

- Your major/favorite subject
- Where you live
- What you do on weekends
- What you're doing later today

Lesson 3 — Game Night

A Model Conversation

Read the conversation. Then listen. Track 05

Olivia: Okay. The next game we're playing is Pictionary. It's a drawing game. Do you want me to explain the rules?

Ted: Please. Is it complicated?

Olivia: No, it's actually very simple. First, you choose a card. It has a word or phrase on it.

Ted: Okay. Then what do I do?

Olivia: You have to draw the word or phrase on this big piece of paper. Your teammates have to try to guess the answer. Guess right, and you get a point.

Ted: That sounds simple.

Olivia: Yes. But remember, no talking! And no writing words.

Ted: Okay, I think I understand.

Olivia: And remember—you have one minute, so draw fast!

B Vocabulary

Fill in the blanks with the correct words from the box.

guess	explain	complicated	simple	teammate
minutes	points	remember	think	understand

1. Let's go. Our train leaves in ten _____.

2. I can't _____ my first day of elementary school. It was a long time ago.

3. The rules of American football are too _____. I don't _____ them.

4. I played soccer in high school, and he was my _____.

5. How many _____ do we need to win?

6. To get a point, you have to _____ the right answer.

7. I'll _____ the rules of the game. It will be quick—they're very _____.

8. This is delicious. I _____ you're a very good cook.

C In Your World

What kinds of games or sports do you play with your friends? List three. Then interview a partner about the games you chose.

1. _____

2. _____

3. _____

Question starters

Do you…?
When…?
How often…?
Why…?
Can you…?

D Grammar

Action verbs and stative verbs

action verbs
Many verbs are action verbs. These are verbs that describe someone or something doing an action, moving, or changing. Examples include *eat*, *play*, and *watch*. These verbs can be used in present continuous sentences: *She **is eating** soup.*

stative verbs
Stative verbs do not describe an action, movement, or change. Examples include *be, remember, understand, love,* and *hate*. These verbs are not usually used in the present continuous. They are often used in the simple present: *This soup **is** cold. I **hate** it!*

verbs with both uses

Some verbs can be both action verbs and stative verbs. For example, *have* is stative when it means to own:
    *He **has** an umbrella.*
 	
But *have* can also mean to experience or to eat. Then it's an action verb and can be used in the present continuous:
    *He**'s having** fun.*
    *We**'re having** breakfast.*

E Grammar Practice

Fill in the blanks with the verbs from the box. Use the correct form for simple present or present continuous.

remember	have	understand	like	need	play

1. My roommates _____ sports, but I hate them.

2. I _____ meeting you for the first time. That was a good day.

3. It's 11:30 p.m., and our neighbor _____ loud music!

4. _____ you _____ the homework? Or should I explain it again?

5. Eric is so tired. He really _____ to sleep more.

6. I hope you're hungry because we _____ turkey for dinner.

F Use the Language

Group activities

In a small group, discuss the activities pictured below. What are the people doing? What do you think of these activities? What do you need when you do these activities?

Lesson 4 — TV Choices

Brief note

The word "on" is used in many expressions about TV shows.
What's on?
There's a good show on at 9:00.
The football game is on channel 12.
It's the best show on TV.

A Model Conversation

Read the conversation. Then listen. 🎧 Track 06

Janice: It's Friday night. Should we go out?

Elena: Actually, I'd rather stay in. I'm tired, and watching TV is more relaxing.

Janice: Well, okay. What's on?

Elena: This is *Kitchen Race*. It's a cooking reality show.

Janice: Oh, no, I'm not a big fan of reality shows.

Elena: They're not my favorite, either. But there isn't much on at 10:00. Would you rather watch a nature show about lions? There's one on now. Or we could watch the news.

Janice: Hmm. I don't like nature shows, and I prefer to read the news, not watch it. What about channel 61 or 23? They usually show old sitcoms at night.

Elena: Do you like sitcoms?

Janice: I love them! I'd always rather watch a funny show than a soap opera. Here, give me the remote.

Elena: Sure. Here you go. Let's see what's on.

Brief note

A "channel" is a TV station.
A: Let's watch Kitchen Race.
B: Okay. What channel is it on?

B Vocabulary

Listen to the words. Then write each under the correct picture. 🎧 Track 07

| news | sitcom | nature show | soap opera | reality show | remote |

_____

_____

_____

_____

_____

_____

C About You

Think of a few more kinds of TV shows not included in part B. Then talk to a partner about what kinds of TV shows you like and don't like.

D Grammar

Brief note

Would rather... than has the same meaning as *prefer... to*.
I'd rather play basketball **than** watch it on TV.
= *I prefer* playing basketball **to** watching it on TV.

Expressing preference with *would rather*

would rather + verb phrase + *than* + verb phrase

Compare two actions with *would rather... than*:
    *I **would rather** play basketball **than** watch it on TV.*
This means you would like the first action more than the second. In questions, you can use *or* to compare two options:
    ***Would** he **rather** go out **or** stay home?*

simpler forms

If we already know what is being compared, we don't need the *than* clause. Just use *would rather*:
    *She doesn't want to watch a reality show. She **would rather** watch a sitcom.*
The short form of *would* is often used:
    *I**'d rather** play basketball.*
    *She**'d rather** watch a sitcom.*

E Grammar Practice

Which do you prefer? Fill in the blanks with the given expressions to make sentences that are true for you. (You can change the order of the given expressions.)

1. I would rather watch _____ than _____. (a reality show, the news)

2. I would rather buy _____ than _____. (food, clothes)

3. I'd rather _____ than _____. (watch TV, play basketball)

4. I'd rather do _____ than _____. (my homework, the laundry)

Now ask a partner about his or her preferences: *Would you rather... or...?*

F Use the Language

Would You Rather...?

1. Brainstorm things that a person can do or experience. Include some things that you would like to do or experience, and some that you would not. Write them in pairs on the lines: for example, *travel by air* or *by car.*

2. Then, with a partner, take turns asking each other to choose between two options. Explain the reasons for your choice and how the options are different.

Would you rather
_____ or _____
_____ or _____
_____ or _____
_____ or _____

15

The Book or the Movie

A Model Conversation

Read the conversation. Then listen. ⊙ Track 08

Brief note

When a movie tells a story from a book, a comic book, a real person's life, etc., we say it "is based on…"
This movie is based on a novel.
It's based on the writer's life.

Maya: How about going to the movies tonight? I'd like to see *Future World*.

Oscar: I don't know. That movie is getting bad **reviews**. Everyone says it's not as good as the **comic book**.

Maya: Oh, it's based on a comic book? I didn't know that. Well, what about *Mr. Amazing*? It's based on a **novel** about a pilot. I heard it's great.

Oscar: Yes, it's a novel by one of my favorite authors, but I'd prefer to read the book rather than see the movie.

Maya: Really? Not me. I prefer seeing a story on the **screen** to reading about it.

Oscar: So, you don't like to read **fiction**?

Maya: Hardly ever. I usually read **non-fiction** about history and science.

Oscar: Well, I love to relax with a good novel on a rainy day. And I really want to read *Mr. Amazing*. Is there another movie we can see?

Maya: Hmm. You like **comedies**, right? How about *Cupcake*? The reviews say that Devin Kurant delivers a fantastic **performance**.

Oscar: Sounds good!

Brief note

Use "be about" to state the topic of something.
*A: What is this novel **about**?*
*B: It's **about** a pilot.*

B Vocabulary

Fill in the blanks with the bold words from the conversation.

1. I don't like to watch movies on my computer. I'd rather see them on a big _____.

2. The movie was a huge success because of the wonderful _____ by all the actors.

3. The *Lord of the Rings* is a famous _____ by the English author J. R. R. Tolkien.

4. This book isn't based on a true story. It's _____.

5. Nick loves to laugh, so all his favorite movies are _____.

6. That book is getting very good _____. They say it's exciting and surprising.

7. The *Spider-Man* movies are based on a popular _____.

8. I'm bored with novels. I would like to read some _____.

C About You

Answer the questions below. Then share your answers with a partner.

1. How many books do you read in a year? _____

2. Write the name of a novel or comic book you like. _____

3. Who is your favorite author? _____

4. Do you prefer to read print (paper) books or e-books? _____

Grammar

Expressing preference and making comparisons with *prefer* and *as... as*

prefer + noun + *to* + noun	*prefer to* + verb (+ *rather than* + verb)

Compare two nouns with *prefer... to*:
   ➤ He **prefers** dogs **to** cats.
 	
We can do the same with gerunds:
   *She **prefers** sleeping late **to** waking up early.*
	Prefer can also be followed by an infinitive:
	   *I don't like to shop in stores. I **prefer to shop** online.*
	
	Use *prefer to* and *rather than* to compare two verb phrases:
	   *I **prefer to** walk **rather than** drive.*

would prefer	
Use *would prefer* when talking about a choice you're making now. *A: Would you like some coffee? B: Thanks, but I **would (I'd) prefer** tea.*	
not as + **adjective** + *as*	

The phrase *not as* + adjective + *as* means *less* + adjective + *than*.
   *The movie is **not as good as** the comic book. = The movie is worse (less good) than than the comic book.*
   The comic book is better than the movie.	

> **Brief note**
>
> If you have no preference, you can use the expression *I like dogs as much as cats.*

Grammar Practice

Answer the questions with complete sentences about your own preferences.

1. Compare showers to baths. Which do you prefer?

    _____.

2. Compare watching sports to playing sports. Which do you prefer?

    _____.

3. Compare vegetables to meat. Which do you prefer?

    _____.

4. Compare reading a book to watching a movie. Which do you prefer?

    _____.

Use the Language

I'd prefer to read...

Work in pairs.

Partner A: Choose one of the books below and suggest it to your partner. Give reasons.

Partner B: Choose a different book below. Explain why you'd prefer to read it. Give reasons. Then switch roles.

A comic book about high school students with special abilities

A funny novel about life in the 1800s in England

A non-fiction book about how to succeed in business

An exciting novel about a woman in the army

Now suggest to your partner a real book or comic book that you like. Say what it is about and give reasons for your suggestion. Then listen and respond to your partner's suggestion.

17

Listen and Complete

Listen to a conversation. While listening, note Monica's problems with her sister, and use the details to fill in the blanks. **Track 09**

1. Monica and her sister usually get along fine, but lately _____.

2. Monica's sister stays awake until _____ anyway. And she's _____ next Saturday.

3. Monica's sister usually _____, and Monica _____.
   But Monica really _____.

4. Monica's sister acts like _____, but _____.

Listen again and make notes on the different things that Monica and her sister do in the apartment. **Track 09**

	Notes

Respond

With a partner, answer the following questions based on the conversation.

1. What is Monica's problem?
2. What does Monica's sister complain about the most?
3. Why doesn't Monica cook more often?
4. What is Ed's advice?
5. Who do you think is right in this argument, Monica or her sister?
6. What do you think Monica should do?

Reminder

Some Module 1 Goals in Unit 1

Put a check mark (✓) next to the things you can do.

_____ Have short conversations with friends, and ask and answer simple questions about familiar topics (for example, hobbies, sports, and music)

_____ Give descriptions on a variety of familiar subjects related to your interests

_____ Understand discussions about daily life and be able to request assistance when needed

Read to Write

Read the magazine article about single-person households.

Living Alone in Seattle

In the US city of Seattle, living alone is popular. About 40% of houses and apartments have only one person in them. Some of these "singles" are living alone because they prefer it. Some just moved to the city. They went there to get a job and didn't bring their families. Others are living alone as the result of divorce. Many are young adults in their first apartments.

Some singles say they prefer living alone because it is quieter and more relaxing. Without roommates, they can cook, sleep, watch TV, read, and play their favorite music at any time. Many singles also spend most of their time outside the home. Others don't like living alone. They say it's not as fun as doing things with other people. They hope to find someone to share their homes with in the future.

Speak to Write

Talk to a partner about how you would feel about living alone. What are some good points and bad points about living alone? What can you do at home when you live alone, and how is this different from living with others?

Now Write

Based on your reading and discussion, prepare to write a paragraph on the subject: Would you rather live alone or live with roommates? Start by writing a short outline within a three-minute time limit. You must think of at least three reasons to support your opinion.

Outline

Now write your paragraph on a separate piece of paper. You have eight minutes. When you are finished, review and edit your paragraph to correct any errors. How many errors did you find?

Lesson 1   Visiting Relatives

A   Model Conversation

Read the conversation. Then listen. Track 10

Brief note
"Thanksgiving" is a US holiday in late November. Families get together to eat a big meal, usually including turkey.

Craig: Hi, Sandra. Happy Thanksgiving.

Sandra: You, too! Are you and Marie on your way?

Craig: No, Marie and the kids are still getting ready. I'm calling to say we'll be a little late.

Sandra: That's okay. Actually, I still have a lot of work to do for dinner. I'm running late, too, because I'm chatting online with my grandchildren in California.

Craig: Oh, how *are* they? And their parents? I miss them.

Sandra: Fantastic. The kids are going to visit next month for a week, so we can look forward to that.

Craig: Great! Nina and John are my only niece and nephew, but I hardly ever see them. Hey, maybe I'll take them to a football game.

Sandra: Yes, they'll love that. So, anyway, what time will you get here?

Craig: We'll be there at about 4:30. Want us to bring anything?

Sandra: No, that's all right. Just be ready to eat a lot.

Craig: We're looking forward to the turkey. I always tell everyone about my mother-in-law's great cooking.

Brief note
A person's "mother-in-law" is the mother of his or her spouse. The word *in-law* can be used with other family words, too. For example, your spouse's brother or your sibling's husband is your *brother-in-law*.

B   Vocabulary

Look at the family tree. Then fill in the blanks with the correct words from the box.

niece   mother-in-law   nephew   grandchildren (*sing.* grandchild)

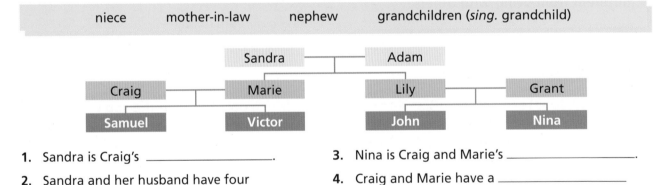

1. Sandra is Craig's _____.

2. Sandra and her husband have four _____.

3. Nina is Craig and Marie's _____.

4. Craig and Marie have a _____ named John.

Match the words and phrases with the correct definitions.

5. be on (one's) way   •
6. look forward to (something) •
7. run late   •
8. miss   •

    • **a.** to think about (a future event) in a happy way
    • **b.** to feel sad because someone isn't with you
    • **c.** to be late getting ready; to be behind schedule
    • **d.** to be going or traveling somewhere

C   About You

Tell a partner about your relatives.

1. Do you have any brothers-in-law or sisters-in-law? What are they like?

2. How many nieces and nephews do your parents have? How many grandchildren? Do they visit your parents often?

3. What do you do when you visit your relatives?

D Grammar

Future tense

future tense with *will* and *be going to*	
We can speak about the future using *will* or *be going to*. Often, you can use either *will* or *be going to*: We'll be a little late. We're going to be a little late.	
will	*be going to*

With *if* (first conditional):
   *If you're late again, mom **will be** upset.*
	For decisions and definite plans made before speaking:
	   *I've packed my suitcase. **I'm going to leave** soon.*

For offers to do something:
   *Those bags look heavy. **I'll help** you.*
	Often, the present continuous has the same meaning:
	   *I've packed my suitcase. **I'm leaving** soon.*

E Grammar Practice

Circle the correct answers.

1. (We're going to / We'll) sell our car. We put an ad in the newspaper.

2. I think maybe (I'm going to / I'll) cook Thanksgiving dinner this year.

3. If you don't study now, you (aren't / won't be) ready for the final exam.

4. They bought a new house in Texas. They (are going to / will) move in July.

5. A: I'm running late for class, and I still have to take the dog for a walk.
    B: No, go to class. (I'll / I'm going to) take him.

F Read to Write

1. Read the email about a family get-together. Underline the future tense verbs.

> Hey, Lucas.
>
> Thanks for inviting me to visit this weekend, but I won't be able to come. Saturday is my sister's 25th birthday, and we're going to give her a big party. It was my future brother-in-law's idea. He and my sister are going to get married in June. On Saturday, we're going to have dinner at her favorite restaurant and then go to her apartment to have cake and hang out. (I'm going to make the cake!) Maybe we'll play some games. It'll be fun. My aunts, uncles, nieces, and nephews will be there. I'm looking forward to it because I don't see them very often. Anyway, let's get together soon. I'll call you.
>
> Alicia

2. Now look at the pictures below. What kind of family get-together would you like to have this weekend? Choose one. Who will come? What will you do? On a separate sheet of paper, write an email to a friend like the one above.

A barbecue at home

A hiking and/or camping trip

A day at the beach

21

A Authentic Text: Online advice column

Read the online advice column. Then discuss the advice with a partner. Do you have any other advice for Stressed Out?

> **✱ Ask Ms. Trudy**
>
>
>
> Dear Ms. Trudy,
> I'm going on a blind date this Friday night. We're going to have a typical dinner-and-movie date, and maybe we'll go to a café. The guy is my best friend's coworker, and she says he's perfect for me. We're both from Australia, and we are studying in the US right now. Also, we have the same major, business, and the same hobby, photography. But it's my first blind date. I'm a little shy with new people. Maybe I won't like him, or he won't like me. I can't stop worrying about it. I might cancel. What's your advice? Help!
> - Stressed Out
>
>
>
> Dear Stressed Out,
> You shouldn't cancel the date. You're right—you may not like him very much, or he may not like you. But that's all right. Try to get to know each other. That will only happen if you relax and be yourself. If you're really nervous, you could ask your friend and her boyfriend to join you on a double date. Perhaps you'll feel more relaxed in a group.
>
> Remember, it's only one evening. So have fun. If it doesn't go well, it's no big deal. And maybe you'll be less nervous on your next blind date.
> - Ms. Trudy
>
> **Brief note**
> "It's no big deal" means it's not important (so don't worry about it).
>
> speedy · 3 hours ago
> 👍 0   👎 0

B Vocabulary

Write the letters of the words and phrases from the box next to the correct definitions.

a. be yourself	b. get to know (someone)	c. cancel	d. double date	e. hobby
f. be stressed out	g. go on a blind date	h. shy	i. worry	j. perfect

1. to learn about a person and become friendly with each other _____
2. to go out with someone you don't know _____
3. to feel afraid that something bad may happen _____
4. to feel a lot of stress _____
5. something you like to do in your free time; a special interest _____

6. to decide not to go to a planned event _____
7. exactly right; having no bad points _____
8. to relax and not worry what others think _____
9. feeling nervous talking to others _____
10. a date that two couples go on together _____

C In Your World

Make a list of three things you would like to do on a blind date and three things you would not like to do. Then compare your ideas with a partner and discuss your reasons.

Me	
I'd like to	**I wouldn't like to**
_____	_____
_____	_____
_____	_____

Grammar

Making predictions and expressing probability with *will* and *be going to*

making predictions
You can make a prediction (give an opinion about the future) using either *will* or *be going to*. It**'ll rain** tomorrow.　　　　　　　　　　　It**'s going to** rain tomorrow.

expressing probability			
maybe	**possibly**	**perhaps**	**probably**
Maybe is often used as a sentence adverb. It means that something is possible but not certain.	*Possibly* can be used after *will* or *be* verbs and as a sentence adverb. It's not used often in speaking.	*Perhaps* is like *maybe*, but it is used more often in writing than in conversation.	*Probably* is stronger than *maybe*, *possibly*, or *perhaps*. It means you are almost sure.
Maybe they are going to see a movie. I will talk to Jim or **maybe** his sister.	He will **possibly** call us tomorrow. He will call us tomorrow, **possibly**.	**Perhaps** you are going to need more money. We will buy some books and **perhaps** a magazine.	She will **probably** get the job. I am **probably** going to stay home on Sunday.

Grammar Practice

Fill in the blanks with the words from the box. If more than one answer is possible, select the one that seems best.

possibly	will	is	maybe	probably

1. I think the guests _____ have a good time.
2. Do you think he _____ going to call you?
3. _____ she will enjoy dinner at an Indian restaurant.
4. She's sick, so she's _____ going to cancel the dinner party.
5. We are _____ going to get a German car, or perhaps an Italian one. We're not sure.

Use the Language

Going on a date

Read the following dating situations. What advice do you have for these people? What will probably happen if they take your advice? What if they don't? Make notes about your advice and predictions on a separate piece of paper.

Emma: For our second date, a guy invited me to an art museum. He knows a lot about art, but I don't. What should I do?

Fred: I went on a blind date at my favorite restaurant. She was very interesting, but she was not nice to our waiter. Should I go out with her again?

Pedro: A girl invited me on a bike ride. I really like her—but I can't ride a bike. I'm worried about telling her. Any advice?

Now compare your ideas with a partner's. Report your ideas to the class.

A   Model Conversation

Read the conversation. Then listen. 🔵 Track 11

Chuck: Hi, everyone. Did you choose a movie for tonight?

Bill: I don't know, what do you and Christine think?

Chuck: Well, I think we should see *Victory Parade*.

Christine: Hmm. I'd rather not. It's an action movie, and it might be really violent.

Sarah: If you hate violent action movies, you must hate horror movies, too, right? Because I'd like to see *House of Rats*.

Christine: Sorry, but no—it looks too scary.

Chuck: Well, *Crazy Quentin* ought to be good. It's the number-one movie in online reviews.

Bill: That's an animated movie, right? Based on a fantasy computer game, I believe. That could be fun.

Chuck: I agree. Oh, wait—we can't see it. It's sold out.

Christine: Hey, I know! Let's see *I Truly Do*. It's a romantic comedy. It should be a good movie for a double date, and I heard it's hilarious.

> **Brief note**
> If a movie is "sold out", it means no more tickets are available.

B   Vocabulary

Write the words from in the box under the correct pictures.

| romantic comedy | fantasy | horror movie | action movie |

_____   _____   _____   _____

Match the words with the correct definitions.

1. animated •   • a. extremely funny
2. violent •   • b. causing fear
3. scary •   • c. telling a story through moving pictures drawn by artists
4. hilarious •   • d. showing people getting hurt

C   About You

List two kinds of movies you like and two kinds you don't like. Give one or two examples of each kind. Then tell a partner and give reasons for your opinions.

		Kinds of movies	Examples (titles)
I like	1.		
	2.		
I don't like	1.		
	2.		

Grammar

Modals of possibility

modals of possibility		
A modal adds meaning to the main verb. Modals of possibility say how sure you are about something.		
meaning	modals	examples
possibility	could, may, might	A: Who's at the door? B: I don't know. It **could** be Jake. Devon **may not** come to the movies with us. I **might** stay home this summer, or I **might** travel. I'm not sure.
strong possibility	should, ought to	This movie **ought to** be good. It's very popular. I'm leaving now, so I **should** be home in ten minutes.
near certainty	must, can't	If you like to laugh, you **must** like comedies. That **can't / must not** be true. It's not possible.

Grammar Practice

Circle the correct answers.

1. All my friends like this restaurant, so it (could / ought to) have good food.

2. Don't touch that snake! It (can't / should) be safe.

3. Eric is still thinking about his plans for tonight. He (might / can't) visit his parents.

4. Kira's car is here, and her bedroom light is on. She (must / could) be home.

5. I'm really excited to see this movie. It (might / should) be hilarious.

6. Check the date on that meat before you cook it. It (may / must) be old.

7. Tim always wants to see fantasy movies. They (should / must) be his favorite.

8. Maybe we shouldn't watch this movie with the kids. It (could / can't) be violent.

Use the Language

What does the future hold?

Fifty years in the future, what will the world be like? Talk about the topics below in small groups. What's possible, and what's not? Try to make at least one prediction about each topic. Ask one member of the group to write your predictions down.

Talk about the possible effects of these changes. Will the world be better or worse? Remember to give reasons.

• Food	• Dating, love, and marriage
• Technology	• Work and jobs
• TV and movies	• Education

Now report your group's most interesting predictions to the class.

Lesson 4 — Nightlife

Brief note

"Feel like" is usually followed by a gerund.
*Do you **feel like** dancing?*

It can also be followed by a noun.
*I **feel like** dessert. = I'd like to eat dessert.*

A — Model Conversation

Read the conversation. Then listen. Track 12

Lawrence: Did you enjoy the concert?

Mary: It was great! I couldn't stop dancing.

Lawrence: Me, neither. Do you feel like dancing more? I know a good club nearby.

Mary: I think I know it, too. Are you talking about Club Blue?

Lawrence: Yes, that's right. It's a fun place.

Mary: Yes, it is. But I'm not sure that I can dance anymore. How about a bar? We can sit down and talk, and maybe have something to eat.

Lawrence: That sounds good. I know one in this neighborhood. My friend is a bartender there, and I'm fairly sure it has no cover charge on weekdays.

Mary: Great!

Lawrence: And it has live music every night. Do you like country music?

Mary: Well… I never listen to it. But I don't mind giving it a try.

Lawrence: Cool. Oh—one more thing. After the band plays, there's karaoke. Can you sing?

Mary: Not at all! I'm really shy in front of big groups!

Lawrence: It's okay. Don't worry. If you don't want to sing, I promise you don't have to.

B — Vocabulary

Write the words from the box next to the correct definitions.

| dance | bartender | live music | promise | feel like | cover charge | bar | concert |

1. _____ to want to do (something) right now

2. _____ money you have to pay to enter a bar, club, etc.

3. _____ to move your body to music

4. _____ music played by a singer or band in front of people, not recorded

5. _____ a person who makes and sells drinks at a bar

6. _____ to say that you will definitely do something

7. _____ a business that mostly sells alcoholic drinks

8. _____ a live music event, usually held in front of a crowd of people

C — In Your World

Think about where you live now or about your hometown. Where can people go to do the following things in the evenings? Which do you like to do? Tell a partner.

Have a romantic date:	Dance:	See a concert:
Eat dinner and hear live music:	Watch or play sports:	Sing karaoke:

26

D Grammar

that clauses

Brief note

The word *that* is often left out of a *that* clause when speaking informally.

that clauses

Some verbs and adjectives can be followed by a *that* clause. A *that* clause contains a noun and verb. *That* clauses are often used with verbs about thoughts, ideas, speech, and giving advice.
    *I think **that** swimming is fun. = I think swimming is fun.*
 	
That clauses can also be used after many adjectives for thoughts, feelings, and possibility.
    *I'm happy **that** you're here. = I'm happy you're here.*

verbs and adjectives which take *that* clauses					
verbs			adjectives		
think	guess	say	certain	aware	likely
believe	know	agree	sure	worried	possible
hope	bet	promise	convinced	hopeful	impossible

Brief note

These verbs include words related to thoughts, ideas, and speech.

Brief note

Adjectives for thoughts, feelings, and possibility are also used with *that*-clauses.

E Grammar Practice

Put the words in order to make sentences.

1. think / you / she / do / come / will _____?

2. doctor / I / rest / says / the / should _____.

3. you / I / won't / living / here / like / am / worried _____.

4. promise / you'll / the / come / party / that / to / me _____.

5. I / that / don't / be / care / angry / she'll _____.

6. be / it / I'll / late / that / is / possible _____.

F Listen to Write

Listen to an advertisement for a new business. What kinds of things can people do there? Put check marks (✓) next to the correct pictures. 🔊 Track 13

Now, with a partner, plan a business in your town. You want people to come to have fun. What kind of business is it? What can people do there? Write a short advertisement like the one you just heard. Share your advertisement with the class. Whose business sounds like the most fun?

A Model Conversation

Read the conversation. Then listen. ⊙ Track 14

Dorothy: I'm bored. Let's get out of the house this weekend.

Ned: Are you sure you want to do that? It's been a long week, and I'm stressed out. I suggest we stay in and rest. We could make a plan for next weekend.

Dorothy: But a day trip could relieve your stress. Why not go for a drive somewhere? We could drive up the coast and walk on the beach, go swimming…

Ned: I agree that sounds fun, but did you see the forecast? There might be a big storm.

Dorothy: If the weather's bad, we can go to the music festival downtown. It starts tomorrow.

Ned: But all of those concerts are outdoors!

Dorothy: Oh. Well, if the weather is nice, let's go to the music festival. If it's bad, we should still go to the beach. I promise it'll be relaxing.

Ned: I guess that's a good plan.

B Vocabulary

Listen to the conversation again. Then match the words with the correct definitions. ⊙ Track 14

1. day trip •
2. outdoors •
3. music festival •
4. relieve •
5. downtown •
6. coast •

• a. a special event with many concerts, usually lasting a few days
• b. the area where the land meets the sea
• c. a trip for only one day
• d. the center of a city or the part with tall buildings, stores, etc.
• e. not inside a building; outside
• f. to make (a bad feeling) better

C In Your World

Where can people take day trips in or near your hometown? Think of three places.

1. _____

2. _____

3. _____

Now talk to a partner. Suggest each of these day trips. Give reasons why your suggestions would be fun trips. Which day trips sound the best?

D Quick Review

Look back at the brief notes in this module.

1. What does *help yourself* mean?

2. Which sentence sounds more formal: "I think they will arrive soon" or "I think that they are going to arrive soon"?

E Grammar

Suggesting activities

In English, there are several common ways to suggest doing something together.	
let's	**suggest (that)**

The most common way to propose something is with *let's* + verb:
   Let's *go!*
	Use *suggest* + *that* clause:
	   I **suggest** *that we go to a museum.*
	   I **suggest** *you reserve a table.*

modal verbs, including *shall*	**questions as suggestions**

Could, should, and *ought to* are often used for suggestions:
   We **could** *see a movie.*
   We **ought to** *visit my parents.*
   You **should** *book a flight.*
	Why not + verb:
	   Why not *go to the mountains?*
	What about + gerund:
	   What about *going to the beach?*
	Why don't you + verb:
	   Why don't you *rest this weekend?*

Brief note

Shall is only used in questions, usually with *we*. It is not commonly used. *Shall we get going?*

F Grammar Practice

Circle the correct answers.

1. Why not (meet / meeting) at a bar to watch the game?

2. I suggest (go / we go) to a concert this weekend.

3. Let's (plan / planning) a day trip to the coast.

4. It's a beautiful day. We (ought to / suggest) have our lunch outdoors.

5. Dancing might relieve your stress. Why don't you (try / trying) it?

6. I want to visit my grandparents this summer. What about (book / booking) a trip there in July?

G Use the Language

Let's go!

Work in groups of two or three students. Plan a weekend trip together using the suggestions below. Each student should choose a different place. Now suggest that place to your group. Suggest things to do there and give reasons why it is the best choice.

A hotel by the ocean
A beautiful but crowded beach
Swimming and water sports

A house by a lake in the forest
Cheap, quiet, relaxing
No TV and no other people

Downtown in a nearby city
Great nightlife
Expensive

Who gave the best reasons? Where should you go? Try to agree. Then tell the class.

A Out on the Town

Read the magazine article about three different districts in one city.

Districts of Berlin

Charlottenburg: If you're interested in fine arts and jazz, then Charlottenburg may be your best choice. Here you can visit the finest museums in the city and a lot of great stores. During the day, you can enjoy a visit to the Berlin zoo. For night owls, there are several exciting jazz clubs to enjoy at night.

> **Brief note**
> A *night owl* is a person who is active at night.

Friedrichshain: If you're looking for great nightlife, you might prefer Friedrichshain. There are karaoke clubs, heavy metal clubs, and many bars with some of the best beers in the world.

Kreuzberg and Schöneberg: Here you will find a casual and relaxed area for shopping and eating out. There are parks, a famous outdoor farmer's market, and many international food choices, from Korean to French to local German restaurants.

B Plan Your Day

Work in small groups. You are going to visit Berlin together. Discuss the districts above. Use the Internet to learn more. Which is the most interesting to you? Talk in detail about the things you could do there and the things you would rather not do. Then, as a group, plan your first day in Berlin. Where will you go, and what will you do?

Morning	
Afternoon	
Evening	

C Reminder

Some Module 1 Goals in Unit 2

Put a check mark (✓) next to the things you can do.

_____ Discuss different things to do, places to go, etc.

_____ Describe plans, arrangements, and alternatives

_____ Understand the main points in short newspaper and magazine articles about current and familiar topics

Listen for Information

Read and then listen to a speaker talk about her plans for the next year. Take notes about things she will do, things she probably will do, and things she might do. 🎧 **Track 15**

> **Woman:** Next year will be a very exciting year for me. I'm graduating high school, and I'm planning to move out of my parents' house. I'm going to attend a university in Florida. I'll probably live on campus with a roommate. But if I get enough money in loans, it's possible I'll live alone in an apartment. I'm going to study photography. I'd like to have a little photo studio of my own. But that probably won't happen for a year or two. I should be able to find a part-time job. If I'm lucky, I may get some work doing wedding photography. I'm going to study hard. I'm excited, but I worry that I won't have any time to relax. Do you think I'll be stressed out? I hope not!

will	probably will	might
_____	_____	_____
_____	_____	_____
_____	_____	_____
_____	_____	_____
_____	_____	_____
_____	_____	_____

Prepare

Now think about a time in your own future. It could be next year, two years from now, or any other time you choose. Write some notes below about what you will do, what you probably will do, and what you might do but aren't sure about yet.

_____

_____

_____

_____

_____

Speak

Using the notes you have prepared, tell a group of your classmates about your future plans. After you've presented some ideas, invite your classmates to ask you questions.

A Vocabulary

Read the sentences. Then choose the correct word or phrase to complete each sentence.

1. I'd rather not read that novel. I don't really like _____.
   a. fiction   b. non-fiction   c. performance

2. Soccer is a game with _____ rules.
   a. hilarious   b. simple   c. scary

3. Should I _____ Sherri to dinner tonight?
   a. invite   b. miss   c. guess

4. Did you make these cookies? Yum—they're _____!
   a. complicated   b. shy   c. delicious

5. Jack says he misses you, and he's _____ to seeing you.
   a. looking forward   b. staying in   c. running late

6. I have two younger _____—a brother and a sister.
   a. siblings   b. parents   c. uncles

7. If you want to meet someone new, you can go on a _____ date with my cousin.
   a. double   b. blind   c. chatting

8. There's going to be a great music _____ here in the first week of June.
   a. sitcom   b. day trip   c. festival

9. Sorry, but I have to _____ our plans. I don't feel well.
   a. remember   b. understand   c. cancel

10. I'm starving! Do you _____ eating?
    a. feel like   b. get to know   c. plan

B Grammar

Look back at the module. Fill in the blanks.

1. Maybe you _____ be less nervous next time.

2. _____ you staying in or going out?

3. Debbie _____ always late!

4. We don't want to go home. We're _____ fun!

5. I would _____ see a sitcom than a reality show.

6. I think we'll have a great time at the nightclub. _____ go!

7. I prefer romantic comedies _____ action movies.

8. Oscar and Maya are _____ to the movies tonight.

9. Ivan thinks he's going _____ win our basketball game.

10. You _____ to take care of yourself.

11. I suggest _____ you try the new Thai restaurant. It's really good.

12. I'll answer your questions. What _____ you want to know?

C Predictions

Talk to a partner about the pictures below, and discuss what you think might happen next. Based on your discussion, write on a separate sheet of paper a few sentences about what could happen.

D What do you want to know?

In groups of two or three students, talk about choosing a roommate. What kinds of people do you prefer, and what do you want to do together? What questions will you ask about a possible roommate before you live together? Write them below.

_____?

_____?

_____?

_____?

_____?

E Interview

Use your notes from above to interview other students in your class. Find out who would be a good roommate for you. Then talk to this student about what he or she will do and what the two of you will do together as roommates.

Fitness and Health

Module 2 Goals

Understand enough of what people say to be able to meet immediate needs

Complete a simple questionnaire or standardized report form using short sentences

Describe past activities, events, and personal experiences (for example, what you did over the weekend)

Make another person understand the points that are most important to you when you explain something

Express yourself reasonably accurately in familiar, predictable situations

Help solve practical problems by saying what you think and asking others what they think

Make arrangements on the telephone or in person (for example, setting up a medical appointment)

Manage unexpected things that could happen on vacation (for example, needing a dentist)

Preview

Look at pages 36 to 61. Complete the exercise.

Write the names of four sports.

_____ _____ _____ _____

On what page do you see medication?

_____

On what pages do you see an injured person?

_____ _____ _____

Write four names of health problems you see.

_____ _____ _____ _____

Discuss

Talk about the questions with a partner.

1. What is the person in the picture doing?

2. Do you have an exercise routine? Why or why not?

3. What's your favorite sport to watch? Why?

4. How often do you get sick? What do you usually do about it?

5. How often do you see the doctor or dentist?

Write

Choose one of the questions from above. Write a couple of sentences to answer it.

_____

_____

_____

Unit 3

Unit 4

Scan the QR code to watch a preview video.

35

Lesson 1 | Watching Sports on TV

A Model Conversation

Read the conversation. Then listen. Track 16

> **Brief note**
> "The Olympics" = the Olympic Games. An "event" is a specific race, game, or other competition in the Olympics.

Oscar: Look, the Olympics are on.

Karen: Oh, good. What events?

Oscar: Right now, it's surfing and diving.

Karen: I don't really like those. When will gymnastics be on?

Oscar: Not today. So, you like watching gymnastics?

Karen: Yeah, it's my favorite summer event. The athletes are able to do such difficult moves and still look graceful.

Oscar: They are pretty amazing.

Karen: As a kid, I dreamed about competing in an Olympic gymnastics event.

Oscar: Really? I wanted to be an Olympic athlete, too, but in skiing. Sadly, I never go skiing these days. And I wasn't good at it, anyway.

Karen: I'm terrible at gymnastics. So I guess we'll never be great athletes.

Oscar: No. But it's still fun to watch them on TV.

> **Brief note**
> Baseball, softball, karate, skateboarding, sport climbing, and surfing are added to the sports program for the Tokyo 2020 Olympics.

B Vocabulary

Listen to the words. Then match each word with the correct definition. Track 17

1. move
2. compete
3. terrible
4. athlete
5. graceful
6. dream

a. a person who does a sport
b. able to move in a beautiful way
c. to think about something you really want to do or be
d. extremely bad
e. to enter a game or contest and try to win
f. an action of the body

C Vocabulary: Olympic sports

Look at the pictures of some Olympic sports. Write the words from the box under the correct pictures.

| gymnastics | diving | figure skating | surfing | skiing |

1. _____
2. _____
3. _____
4. _____
5. _____

D About You

As a kid, did you dream of being an athlete? If yes, in what sport? If not, what did you dream of being?

Think about your answers to the questions. Then share them with a partner.

E Grammar

Gerunds and infinitives

Brief note

The phrase *be able to* means *can*. But it can be used after a modal verb. You cannot use *can* after another modal verb.
(✓) *She might be able to compete in the Olympics.*
(X) *She might can compete in the Olympics.*

gerunds (verb-*ing*)	infinitives (*to* + verb)
As the subject of a sentence or after the *be* verb: **Swimming** *is my favorite sport.* *My favorite sport is* **swimming**.	After certain verbs (for example, *like, choose, agree, want*): *We* **agreed to meet** *on Sunday.* **Try to eat** *more vegetables.*
After a preposition: *He is good* **at writing** *in English.* *I'm interested* **in skiing**.	After some adjectives (for example, *fun, able, nice*): *The X Games are* **fun to watch**. *The athletes are* **able to do** *graceful moves.*
After certain verbs (for example, *like, enjoy, mind, practice*): *I* **enjoy watching** *the Olympics.* *Would you* **mind closing** *the window?*	After *know how*: *I* **know how to swim** *well.* *Do you* **know how to play** *the guitar?*
After *go* (for example, *shopping, dancing*, and some other activities): *Let's* **go shopping/surfing**. *We're* **going swimming/running**.	

Brief note

Some verbs can be followed by either a gerund or an infinitive. They include *like, love, hate, start,* and *begin*.

F Grammar Practice

Circle the correct answers. If both answers are possible, circle both.

1. I have to practice (to sing / singing) this song.

2. Are you good at (to get / getting) to know new people?

3. Patrick wasn't able (to find / finding) a seat.

4. Does the teacher want (to talk / talking) to me?

5. You don't have to walk to school. I don't mind (to drive / driving) you.

6. Do you know how (to cook / cooking)?

7. We usually go (to run / running) in the morning.

8. My sister loves (to go / going) surfing in the summer.

9. That actor is fun (to watch / watching) on the screen.

10. The class started (to laugh / laughing).

G Use the Language

Watching sports

Talk with one or two partners about their favorite athlete, their favorite sport to watch, and the reasons for their choices. Take notes and fill in the chart.

Name		
Favorite athlete		
Reason(s)		
Favorite sport to watch		
Reason(s)		

Share your chart with the class. Who gave the most surprising answers? The most interesting reasons?

A   Model Conversation

Read the conversation. Then listen. 🎧 Track 18

Hailey: Hey, Ben. You weren't in class yesterday—were you sick?

Ben: No, I'm fine. I went to cheer for my brother Ethan's college basketball team. It was such an excellent game.

Hailey: Oh, yeah? What happened?

Ben: They were behind by one point, and there were five seconds left. Then Ethan got the ball and scored. It was incredible.

Hailey: Wow! So, I guess your brother's a good player?

Ben: The best on the team—and it's a good team. I highly recommend you go and watch sometime. In fact, I'm going to their game on Wednesday, if you're free.

Hailey: I am. What time?

Ben: It starts at 7:00 p.m., but we'd better show up early to get good seats. Can you meet me here at 6:15?

> **Brief note**
>
> Use the preposition "on" to talk about being part of a team.
> *My friend Claire is **on** that team.*

B   Vocabulary

Write the words from the box next to the correct definitions.

basketball	excellent	show up	left	score	second	behind

1. _____ to get a point or points in a game

2. _____ 1/60 of a minute

3. _____ to arrive at a place

4. _____ having fewer points than the other person or team in a game

5. _____ extremely good; fantastic

6. _____ a sport in which players score by throwing a ball through a net (basket)

7. _____ not used or finished yet; remaining

Match the parts to make sentences.

8. I waited for her for an hour, but she didn't   •
9. Oh, we missed the game. There's only   •
10. They're not going to win. They're behind   •
11. If you're very tall, people might think you're   •
12. I suggest you ask Rita to be on your team. She's •
13. Our basketball team played well. We scored   •

  • a. by twenty-two points.
  • b. an excellent athlete.
  • c. ninety points.
  • d. one minute left.
  • f. show up.
  • g. good at basketball.

C   About You

Are you punctual? Do you arrive early to events or are you always late? Talk to a partner about your time management skills.

Grammar

Suggestions and advice with gerunds, infinitives, modals, and *that* clauses

suggestions and advice with gerunds and infinitives	
I suggest / I recommend + gerund	
*I **recommend watching** the basketball game on TV.* *I **suggest going** on the weekend.* Using *I suggest/recommend* + gerund sounds more formal than using infinitives or modal verbs.	
be sure / it's a good idea + infinitive	
Be sure to go to a game.	**It's a good idea to get** tickets early.
strong advice with the modal *had better*	suggestions with *that* clauses
subject + (*had*) *better* + verb	*I suggest/recommend* + *that* clause
We**'d better show up** early to get good seats. = We **better show up** early to get good seats.	I **recommend (that)** she go and watch the game. = I **suggest (that)** she go and watch the game.

Brief note

Informally, people often leave out *had*.

Brief note

In the *that* clause, use the base form of the verb with all subjects:
(✓) *I suggest (that) she/he/it go...*
(X) *I suggest (that) she/he/it goes...*

Grammar Practice

Fill in the blanks with the correct words from the box.

better	idea	sure	suggest	bring	inviting	that

1. I _____ that you stay. There are only ten minutes left in the game.

2. Be _____ to see the college volleyball team sometime!

3. You'd better _____ a warm coat. It's going to be cold later.

4. I recommended _____ lots of friends to the game.

5. It's a good _____ to watch the game on TV.

6. I recommend _____ we sit near the front.

7. Jim's team had _____ practice more. They never win any games.

Use the Language

Let's catch a game!

Go online and research a sporting event that will happen soon in your area. Then suggest to a partner that you both attend and explain why it would be fun. Discuss what you need to do to go to the event. Share your plans with the class.

A   Model Conversation

> **Brief note**
>
> "Work out" is a verb. *Workout* is a noun.
> *Did you* **work out** *today?*
> *How was your* **workout**?

Read the conversation. Then listen. 🔊 Track 19

Sophia: Excuse me. I just worked out here for the first time, and I'm interested in joining the gym.

Marc: Excellent. Let's talk about your options. You can buy a two-month, six-month, or one-year membership.

Sophia: Hmm. I'll take the two-month membership. I'll be studying in the fall. I probably won't be working out often.

Marc: Okay. And what are your fitness goals?

Sophia: I don't want to lose weight. I just want to get in shape. I'd like to be stronger and have more energy.

Marc: Those are good goals. I recommend that you lift weights and join a yoga class. Yoga classes are included with your membership.

Sophia: Maybe I will try it. Are there any classes today?

Marc: No, but I'll be teaching yoga all afternoon tomorrow, from 1:00 to 5:00. Try to stop by then.

B   Vocabulary

Read the words. Then listen to the definitions. Write the letters of the definitions next to the correct words. Then look up the definitions in the dictionary. 🔊 Track 20

1. work out _____   2. lose weight _____   3. join _____   4. get in shape _____

Fill in the blanks with the correct words from the box.

energy	fitness	strong	membership	lift weights

5. I recommend getting a three-month _____ to a gym if you want to get in shape.

6. I don't have much _____ in the morning. I usually feel tired.

7. Let's ask Gary to move the sofa. He's really _____.

8. If you _____ every week, you will get stronger.

9. Mika works at a gym, so she knows a lot about _____.

C   Comprehension

Listen to the model conversation again. Then answer the questions with complete sentences. 🔊 Track 19

1. What did Sophia do for the first time?   A: She _____.
2. What membership will Sophia get?   A: She will _____.
3. What will she be doing in the fall?   A: She will be _____.
4. What are her fitness goals?   A: She wants _____,

_____, _____.

5. What does Marc recommend?   A: He recommends that _____.
6. What will Marc be doing tomorrow afternoon?   A: He'll be _____.

Grammar

Future continuous tense

future continuous tense	
You can use the future continuous to talk about future actions that continue for a period of time. It is formed with *will / be going to* + *be* + verb-*ing*.	
a future action lasting for a while	
with *will*	with *be going to*
We'll **be studying** in Canada for three months. She **won't be working** Friday evening. **Will** you **be working** on weekdays?	I'm **going to be teaching** yoga this afternoon. They're **not going to be practicing** next weekend. **Are** you **going to be studying** for the test tonight?
a future action happening at a specific time	
Meet me after class. I'll **be waiting** outside.	They **aren't going to be working** on Sunday.

Grammar Practice

Circle the correct answers.

1. I'll (be working / working) out tomorrow at 5:00 a.m.

2. You're going (be / to be) waiting in line for a long time.

3. When you come home, I'll (going to be / be) making dinner.

4. We aren't (going to / will) be sitting in class all day.

5. (Will / Are) you going to be staying with relatives during the break?

6. Will (they be / they) studying all night?

Use the Language

What will you be doing?

You want to get in shape, so you'll be working out and playing sports a lot on weekends. Fill in the chart with different kinds of exercise or sports. Note the time when you will be doing each. (Leave some free time!)

	Fitness Schedule		
	Morning	**Afternoon**	**Evening**
Saturday	Time: From to	Time: From to	Time: From to
Sunday	Time: From to	Time: From to	Time: From to

Work with a partner. You want to hang out with him or her this weekend. Ask each other questions about what you will be doing this weekend at different times. Try to find a time when you are both free to meet. Find out if you will be doing any of the same exercises or sports. Suggest doing something together.

Lesson 4 — Fitness Tips

A — Authentic Text: Workout guide

Read the text. Then listen. 🔊 Track 21

Brief note
The phrase "get your money's worth" means to get a good deal. It means you are happy and don't feel that you paid too much money.

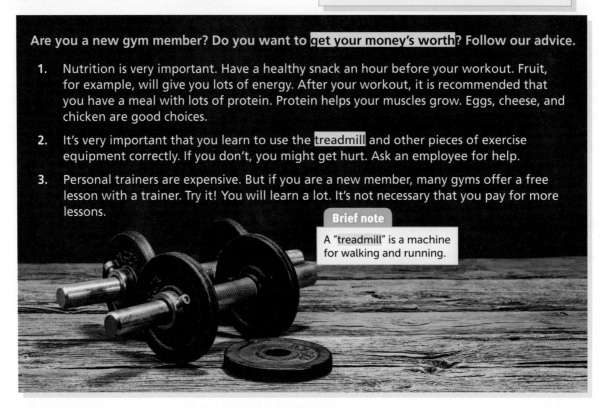

Are you a new gym member? Do you want to get your money's worth? Follow our advice.

1. Nutrition is very important. Have a healthy snack an hour before your workout. Fruit, for example, will give you lots of energy. After your workout, it is recommended that you have a meal with lots of protein. Protein helps your muscles grow. Eggs, cheese, and chicken are good choices.

2. It's very important that you learn to use the treadmill and other pieces of exercise equipment correctly. If you don't, you might get hurt. Ask an employee for help.

3. Personal trainers are expensive. But if you are a new member, many gyms offer a free lesson with a trainer. Try it! You will learn a lot. It's not necessary that you pay for more lessons.

Brief note
A "treadmill" is a machine for walking and running.

B — Vocabulary

Write the words from the box under the correct pictures.

| get hurt | personal trainer | protein | exercise equipment | muscle |

_____   _____   _____   _____   _____

Match the words with the correct definitions.

1. necessary   •   • a. needed
2. healthy   •   • b. the process of eating the right kinds of food to be healthy
3. free   •   • c. available without paying money; at no cost
4. important   •   • d. good for your body
5. nutrition   •   • e. having a lot of value; serious

C — About You

Do you worry about your nutrition? What are your eating habits? Share with a partner. Discuss who eats healthier and why.

D Grammar

Empty *it* and *that* clauses

Brief note

The subject in these sentences is called "empty *it*" because *it* does not stand for a noun. Other kinds of sentences with empty *it* include:
A: *What time is it?*   B: *It's 3:30.*
A: *How far is it to the gym?*   B: *It's two kilometers.*

It is + adjective + *that* clause
It is + adjective + *that* clause can be used with certain adjectives to talk about suggestions, rules, and recommendations. These adjectives include *recommended, important, necessary,* and *required*.

Having a meal with protein is recommended.	= ***It is recommended that*** you have a meal with protein.
Learning to use the exercise equipment is important.	= ***It's important that*** you learn to use the exercise equipment.
Paying for more lessons is not necessary (for you).	= ***It's not necessary that*** you pay for more lessons.
Paying for more lessons is not required (for her).	= ***It is not required that*** she pay for more lessons.

You can also use *it is* + adjective + *that* clause with some other adjectives about opinions. These adjectives include *good, great, amazing, terrible,* and *possible*.

It's possible that I'll join a gym.	***It's great that*** he's eating healthy foods.

Brief note

In *that* clauses about suggestions, rules, etc., use the base form of the verb with all subjects. In these sentences, you cannot leave out *that*.
(✓) *It's important that **he/she learn** to use the exercise equipment.*
(X) *It's important he/she learns to use the exercise equipment.*

E Grammar Practice

Rewrite the sentences using *It's* and a *that* clause.

1. Drinking water on a hot day is important. _____

2. Talking to your doctor is necessary. _____

3. Taking long walks is recommended. _____

4. He never eats vegetables. That's terrible. _____

F Use the Language

Health and fitness questionnaire

Complete the following questionnaire about your health and fitness. Then ask a partner the questions and write his or her answers in short sentences. Do you have similar answers? How are your answers different?

Me	My Partner (Name: _____)
1. What kind of exercise do you like?	1. What kind of exercise do you like?
2. How good is your health? (Circle one.) Excellent Good Average Bad	2. How good is your health? (Circle one.) Excellent Good Average Bad
3. How often do you eat healthy meals? Always Usually Sometimes Never	3. How often do you eat healthy meals? Always Usually Sometimes Never
4. What are some healthy foods?	4. What are some healthy foods?
5. How could you improve your health?	5. How could you improve your health?

Share some recommendations about how to live a healthier life with your partner. Do you think these are good recommendations? Share your ideas with the class.

A Model Conversation

Read the conversation. Then listen. Track 22

> **Brief note**
>
> "What's the matter?" means "What's wrong?"

Trainer: What's the matter, Miguel? Did you hurt your shoulder?

Miguel: Yeah, I tried to lift that 40 kg weight pretty fast. I guess that wasn't smart. It really hurts.

Trainer: Uh-oh. Can you lift your arm?

Miguel: Yeah. I can, but it's very painful.

Trainer: Okay, then stop moving it. It might get even worse. I'll get a bandage. Then you'd better go home and put ice on it.

Miguel: Is that necessary? Maybe the pain will stop.

Trainer: No, it's possible that it's a serious injury. Rest the arm and take some pain relievers. If it isn't a lot better after three days, you'll need to see a doctor.

> **Brief note**
>
> The verb "put" needs two things after it: a direct object and an adverb or a prepositional phrase of location.
> (✓) *Put ice on your shoulder. / Put ice there.*
> (X) *Put ice.*

B Vocabulary

Match the words with the correct definitions.

1. shoulder •
2. serious •
3. painful •
4. put •
5. pain reliever •
6. bandage •
7. ice •
8. injury •

• a. frozen water
• b. causing (a part of the body) to hurt
• c. possibly dangerous
• d. a long piece of cloth to cover a hurt part of the body
• e. medicine for making pain stop
• f. the top of the arm
• g. the act of getting hurt; damage to part of the body
• h. to cause to be in a specific place

C Vocabulary: Body parts

Fill in the empty blanks with words from the box.

| ankle | elbow | knee | neck | wrist | forehead |

1. ___
2. ___
   stomach
3. ___
   thigh
4. ___
   calf
5. ___

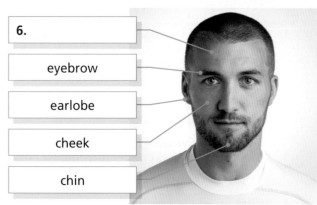

6. ___
   eyebrow
   earlobe
   cheek
   chin

D About You

Think of a time you were injured. What did you hurt? How did the injury happen? Was it painful? What did you do about it? Tell your partner.

Grammar

Intensifiers

intensifiers
Use intensifiers to make the meaning of adjectives stronger. Sometimes you want to emphasize how big, small, great, painful, etc., something is. The intensifier can be a word or a phrase. It comes before the adjective: *Their house is **really** big.*   *The soup is **a little** salty.*   *Rock climbing is **quite** difficult.*
common intensifiers

a bit / a little	pretty / fairly / quite	so / really / very / super	extremely
←--→
least strong			*strongest*

comparing using intensifiers
Some intensifiers (*even, so much, a lot*) can be used with comparative adjectives. Other intensifiers cannot.
My elbow feels **a lot better** now.   It's **even hotter** today than yesterday.   He's **so much taller** than his brother.

> **Brief note**
>
> Most of these intensifiers can be used in front of an adjective + noun. However, *a bit, a little,* and *so* cannot. They can only be used in front of an adjective alone.
> (✓) *It's a **pretty** expensive gym.*
> (✓) *It's **a bit** expensive.*
> (X) *It's a bit expensive gym.*

Grammar Practice

Add an intensifier to make sentences that are true for you. Share with a partner. Do you and your partner agree?

1. Working out every day is _____ hard.

2. Cooking healthy meals every day is _____ difficult.

3. Cleaning the house is _____ boring.

4. Watching the Olympics is _____ fun.

5. Reading comic books is _____ relaxing.

6. Going on a blind date is _____ stressful.

Use the Language

What's the matter?

Look at the pictures. Imagine what is happening in each situation. What problems do the people in the pictures have and what should they do next? On a separate piece of paper, write a conversation between you and the person in each picture. Then show your conversations to a partner. Practice the conversations together. Then choose the best one and present it to the class.

Email

Read Jessica's email. Then answer the questions.

Dear Becky,

Happy New Year! How are you? I've been good, but I'm busy at college. I joined the basketball team this year! We're actually fairly good. But being on the team is really tough. We practice three times a week and go to the gym twice a week. I started to lift weights and take yoga classes. Sometimes, I even go swimming. My schedule is pretty busy but quite fun, too. I also have a personal trainer. He will be helping me get in shape and teaching me to prepare a meal plan. It's cool that the school helps us with our fitness routine.

Some bad news: last week, I hurt my knee. It's still a little painful. My trainer recommended that I rest for a few days—which is okay with me! The Olympic basketball team will be visiting us next week! I'm pretty excited about that.

But enough about me. What will you be doing over the break?

Write back soon,
Jessica

---

1. What team did Jessica join at her college? _____

2. What does Jessica do at the gym? _____

3. What will her personal trainer be doing? _____

4. What happened last week? _____

5. What did her trainer recommend? _____

6. What is going to be happening next week? _____

Write

Write an email back to Jessica on a separate piece of paper. Give your email to a partner to read and check. Then read your email out loud to the class.

Reminder

Some Module 2 Goals in Unit 3

Put a check mark (✓) next to the things you can do.

_____ Understand enough of what people say to be able to meet immediate needs

_____ Complete a simple questionnaire or standardized report form using short sentences

_____ Express yourself reasonably accurately in familiar, predictable situations

_____ Help solve practical problems by saying what you think and asking others what they think

---

Prepare

Look at a person's fitness routine. Work with a partner. One of you is Person #1, and the other is Person #2. Look at your chart and cover the other chart. Ask your partner questions about each day and fill in the missing information in your chart. Pretend that today is Monday.

Person #1

Monday (TODAY)	Tuesday	Wednesday	Thursday	Friday	Saturday	Sunday
Gym: 30 minutes treadmill, lifting weights	Swimming: 30 minutes	Gym: 25 minutes yoga, lifting weights			Gym: 20 minutes treadmill, 20 minutes yoga	

Person #2

Monday (TODAY)	Tuesday	Wednesday	Thursday	Friday	Saturday	Sunday
Gym: 30 minutes treadmill, lifting weights			Rest	Basketball club		Gym: 20 minutes exercise bike, 20 minutes swimming

Speak to Write

What do you think of the person's fitness routine? Do you have any suggestions or advice for him or her? With the same partner, discuss what you think he or she can change or add. Share your ideas with the class.

Now Write

Write your own weekly fitness routine in the chart below. Then share it with another partner. What does your partner think of your routine? Next, ask your partner to make a meal plan for you. How does the meal plan help you reach your fitness goals?

		Monday	Tuesday	Wednesday	Thursday	Friday	Saturday	Sunday
Exercise Plan								
Meal Plan	(breakfast)							
	(lunch)							
	(dinner)							

Lesson 1	Making a Doctor's Appointment

A Model Conversation

Read the conversation. Then listen. Track 23

Receptionist: Dr. Jackson's office. How can I help you?

Patient: Hello. I'd like to make an appointment to see the doctor.

Receptionist: Have you been here before?

Patient: Yes, I have.

Receptionist: Okay. What's your name and date of birth?

Patient: Samuel Chapman, May 13th, 1990.

Receptionist: And what's the reason for your visit?

Patient: I've had a nasty headache since last week. I'm not sure what to do. I've tried different medications, but they haven't helped.

Receptionist: Sounds like the flu. Do you have any other symptoms—vomiting or trouble breathing?

Patient: No, just the pain.

Receptionist: Have you ever experienced a similar headache before?

Patient: No. I'm usually very healthy. Could I see the doctor today?

Receptionist: Yes, we've just had a cancellation. Can you come at 3:00?

> **Brief note**
> A "symptom" is any feeling or change in the body that happens when you are sick.

B Vocabulary

Look at the pictures and listen to the words. Then write the correct word under each picture. Track 24

patient	illness	headache	medication/medicine	vomit

_____ _____ _____ _____ _____

Match the words with the correct definitions.

1. trouble breathing •   • a. the act of stopping something that has been planned
2. nasty •   • b. alike; seeming the same or almost the same
3. flu •   • c. being unable to breathe (take air into the body) easily
4. cancellation •   • d. very bad; very serious or painful
5. similar •   • e. an illness like a cold, but more serious

C Comprehension

Read the statements about the conversation and circle true or false. Check your answers with a partner.

1. Samuel is Dr. Jackson's patient.	true	false
2. He hasn't taken any medicine yet.	true	false
3. He has several symptoms.	true	false
4. He will be able to see the doctor this afternoon.	true	false

Grammar

Present perfect tense

Brief note

For regular verbs, the past participle is the same as the simple past form. Some verbs are irregular.
For more about past participles, see Grammar Reference, p. 121.

present perfect		
You use the present perfect tense to talk about past events that have a connection to the present. The form of the present perfect is *have/has* + past participle.		
meaning	**common expressions**	**examples**
past state/action that continues to the present	*for* + period of time *since* + point in time	She **has worked** here for three years. I**'ve had** a terrible headache since last week.
experience	*before, ever, never, once, twice, ~ times*	A: **Have** you (ever) **been** there before? B: Yes, I **have**. / No, I**'ve** never **been** there. I**'ve tried** medications, but they **haven't helped**.
change over time	*since* + point in time	The baby**'s grown** so much since last month!
completed actions	*already, yet*	I**'ve** already **finished** my project. **Have** you **started** yours yet?
recent events with an effect on the present; news	*just*	He**'s broken** his leg. We**'ve** just **had** a cancellation.

Grammar Practice

Underline the errors and rewrite the sentences correctly using the present perfect tense.

1. I've feel sick since last night. _____

2. He has had a headache for this morning. _____

3. Have you went to the hospital? _____

4. Has you just booked an appointment with the doctor? _____

5. Jake has broke his leg. _____

6. She hasn't saw the doctor yet. _____

Use the Language

Sick day

Tell a partner about the last time you were sick and what you did to feel better.

Take notes on your partner's story. Then write a short story summarizing your partner's sick day.

Notes: Partner's story	Short story

A Model Conversation

Read the conversation. Then listen. 🔘 Track 25

Doctor: Hi, Robin. What seems to be the problem?

Patient: Well, doctor, I've had nausea for the last two days. I can't keep anything down.

Doctor: Have you had any other symptoms? Headache? Fever? Body aches? Anything like that?

Patient: Yes, I had a stomachache and body aches yesterday. They're gone now. I feel a little better, but I still can't eat.

Doctor: Hmm. Have you eaten any bad-tasting food recently—especially chicken, eggs, or seafood?

Patient: I don't think so. I had lunch the other day at a seafood restaurant, but the food tasted fine.

Doctor: Well, it sounds like food poisoning to me, but it's hard to know for sure. You're already getting better, so my advice is to rest and drink lots of water or juice.

Patient: You can't give me a prescription?

Doctor: Sorry, the only cure for food poisoning is time. You can buy pills for the nausea at any pharmacy, but it might not help. If your nausea isn't gone in a few days, then call me again.

> **Brief note**
>
> "I can't keep anything down" means you keep vomiting whenever you eat anything.

B Vocabulary: Symptoms

Listen to the list of symptoms. Then write the letter of the correct definition next to each. 🔘 Track 26

1. nausea _____
2. sore throat _____
3. body aches _____
4. cough _____
5. runny nose _____
6. fever _____
7. congestion _____
8. allergy _____

a. a high body temperature

b. a feeling of sickness; wanting to vomit

c. having liquid come from your nose

d. pain all over the body

e. a painful feeling in your throat (inside your neck)

f. a blocked nose; trouble breathing through your nose

g. getting ill from a specific thing (a food, an animal, a medication, etc.)

h. to push air out suddenly from your throat with a noise

C Vocabulary in Context

Listen to the words and their definitions. Practice saying the words out loud. Then fill in the blanks with the correct words. 🔘 Track 27

cure: a way to stop a medical problem

food poisoning: illness from eating spoiled (not fresh) or incorrectly cooked food

gone: no longer there; (of a symptom) having stopped

pill: a small, circle-shaped piece of medication

prescription: a note from a doctor to a pharmacist about medication for a patient

1. Take one _____ three times a day with meals.

2. The doctor gave me a _____ for some headache medication. Now my pain is _____!

3. There is no _____ for a cold, but medicine can help with the symptoms.

4. Always be sure to cook chicken well, or you might get _____.

Grammar

Present perfect vs. simple past

present perfect vs. simple past		
present perfect	Use the present perfect to talk about an action or state that is not finished. It has a connection to the present.	
	I've lived here for three years. (I moved here three years ago, and I still live here.)	
	Use the present perfect when the time of a past action is not important or not known.	
	I haven't had the flu for a long time.	We've already seen that movie.
simple past	Use the simple past to talk about an action or state that happened in the past and is finished.	
	I lived there for three years. (I do not live there anymore. I have moved.)	
	Use the simple past with past time expressions.	
	I had the flu last week, but I'm better now.	We saw that movie yesterday.

Grammar Practice

Fill in the blanks with the correct forms of the verbs in parentheses.

1. My dad _____ (feel) terrible last night.

2. You _____ (forget) to take your pills this morning.

3. _____ you ever _____ (see) this doctor before?

4. I'm very healthy. I _____ (not get) sick for years!

5. She _____ (have) an allergy to cats since she was about 4 years old.

6. I _____ (take) that medicine for a week and then stopped.

7. He _____ (have) a severe cough yesterday, but it's gone now.

8. Maria _____ already _____ (tell) the doctor about her sore throat and body aches.

Use the Language

I have never told a lie!

Write ten sentences about yourself. Some sentences should be true, and others should be lies. Write about things in the past, or things that started in the past and continue until now.

Then get in small groups. Share your sentences with the group. Your group will guess if your sentence is true or a lie. Each correct guess gets one point. The person with the most points at the end is the winner.

Ten things about me	
1.	6.
2.	7.
3.	8.
4.	9.
5.	10.

A Model Conversation

Read the conversation. Then listen. Track 28

Hygienist: Hi, Fiona. Have you rinsed with the mouthwash?
Patient: Yes, I have.
Hygienist: Let's have a look. Hmm. How often do you floss?
Patient: Um, once a week, maybe.
Hygienist: That's not often enough. You need to do it every day to keep your gums healthy.
Patient: I don't like it, though. It makes my gums bleed.
Hygienist: That's common if you don't do it often. Now, I'd like you to promise that you'll floss more often.
Patient: I know, you're right. I promise.
Hygienist: Good. Now. Well, your teeth don't look too bad. There's a little staining, and I think you do have one cavity. The X-ray will tell us for sure if you'll need a filling. Dr. Marino will be here in just a moment to tell you.
Patient: Okay, thanks.
Dentist: Hello, Fiona. It's good to see you. I've got your X-ray right here. It's been too long since your last visit. Now, let's have a look.

Brief note
A "cavity" is a hole in a tooth that must be filled.

B Vocabulary

Listen to the words. Then write each word under the correct picture. Track 29

| filling | hygienist | staining | gums | floss | mouthwash | rinse | X-ray |

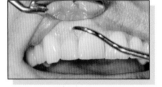   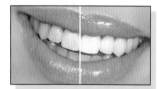

_____ _____ _____ _____

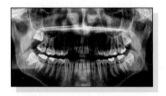   

_____ _____ _____ _____

C Vocabulary in Context

Fill in the blanks with the correct words from the box to complete the summary.

Fiona is at the ⓐ _____ office. The hygienist is checking her
ⓑ _____. He asks her if she has been ⓒ _____ every
day. Fiona doesn't floss often enough. She says that it makes her gums
ⓓ _____. The hygienist says that is ⓔ _____. He also
thinks Fiona's teeth don't look ⓕ _____. But there is a little
ⓖ _____, and she might have one ⓗ _____.

cavity	flossing
common	dentist's
bleed	staining
teeth	too bad

D Grammar

too and *enough*; *want / would like* + object + infinitive

too and *enough*	*want / would like* + object + infinitive
Too is an adverb meaning "more than what is needed or wanted." It comes before an adjective or adverb.	You use the structure *want / would like* + object + infinitive to talk about something you want someone to do.
It's been **too** long since your last visit. I can't eat the soup. It's **too** hot.	My mom **wants my brother to go** to the dentist. **I'd like you to promise** you'll floss more often.
Enough is an adverb meaning "equal to what is needed; to the necessary degree." It comes after an adjective or adverb.	
That's not often **enough**. She can't drive a car. She's not old **enough**.	

> **Brief note**
>
> *Too* and *enough* have opposite meanings.
> The soup is **too** hot. = The soup isn't cool **enough**.
> She's not old **enough**. = She's **too** young.

> **Brief note**
>
> *Would like* is more polite than *want*.

E Grammar Practice

Read each pair of sentences. Choose the correct sentence. Compare your answers with a partner. Can you explain why the other sentence is wrong? Discuss with your partner.

1. a. I like you to lie down on the chair, please.
    b. I'd like you to lie down on the chair, please.

2. a. This sweater is too big. I need a smaller one.
    b. This sweater is big enough. I need a smaller one.

3. a. I want you to book an appointment for me.
    b. I want you book an appointment for me.

4. a. Your teeth are clean enough.
    b. Your teeth are enough clean.

5. a. He's like you to come in next week.
    b. He'd like you to come in next week.

6. a. She wants you using mouthwash every day.
    b. She wants you to use mouthwash every day.

7. a. The weather doesn't look too bad today.
    b. The weather doesn't look bad enough today.

8. a. I'd like you to helping me with this, please.
    b. I'd like you to help me with this, please.

F Use the Language

What seems to be the problem?

Work with a partner and role-play a visit to the doctor's office.

- First, decide who plays the patient and who plays the doctor.
- Then take a few minutes to think about your symptoms (if you are the patient) and questions to ask (if you are the doctor). Use the Medical Report to take notes.
- Role-play the conversation. Try to agree on what the patient's problem is and what to do about it.
- Perform your conversation for the class.

> **Brief note**
>
> *Physician* is another word for a medical doctor.

Medical Report		
Patient's name (last, first, middle)	Birth date	Visit date
Physician	Date of report	Next appointment
Symptoms/Diagnosis		

53

A   Authentic Text: Therapist blog

Read the story. Then listen. 🎧 Track 30

THERAPIST BLOG

People don't usually think about their mental health, but they should! Your mind is just as important as your body. Stress and other emotional problems can be as serious as a physical illness or injury. That's why I became a school psychologist. As a therapist, my job is to listen to students' problems—academic, emotional, and social—and to counsel students on how to deal with their problems.

For instance, just last month, I started to help a student with a lot of stress. Her classes are very difficult, so she was spending a lot of time in the library. She wasn't sleeping well, and she always felt tired. She was losing weight, and even her relationships with friends were getting worse. She was fighting with her roommate every night. To help her, I asked her to visit me regularly. During our meetings, I teach her how to meditate and other ways to relax. We also talk about her problems. Now she says she has already started to sleep better.

🤝 5   22   👍 435   👎 43

B   Vocabulary

Listen to the words. Then write each word next to the correct definition. 🎧 Track 31

mental	emotional	physical	therapist	social	counsel	regularly	meditate

1. _____ to give advice to

2. _____ involving being with other people or relationships with other people

3. _____ having to do with your feelings; often showing strong feelings

4. _____ very often or every day, week, month, etc.

5. _____ having to do with your mind: your thoughts, attitude, beliefs, etc.

6. _____ to spend time thinking quietly, often to relax

7. _____ having to do with the body and not the mind

8. _____ a person who helps with illnesses of the mind

C   Vocabulary Comprehension

Fill in the blanks with the correct words from part B.

1. Dennis is shy, so he doesn't like going to _____ events alone.

2. Exercising _____ is good for both your mental and your _____ health.

3. She had a serious illness as a child, so she knows how to _____ sick children.

4. To be a(n) _____, you must want to help people, and you must be a good listener.

5. Erica is not a very _____ person. She never seems really happy or really upset.

6. When I have a problem, I like to sit and _____. It often helps me work out the problem.

D Grammar

Past continuous tense; *when* clauses

past continuous	*when* clauses
Use the past continuous to talk about an action that continued for some time in the past. The form is *was/were* + verb-*ing*.	You can use *when* clauses with the past continuous to talk about something that interrupted or happened during a continuous action. You use the simple past in the *when* clause.
a past action that lasted for a while	
She **was spending** a lot of time in the library. He **wasn't sleeping** well last week.	You were cooking dinner from 6 to 7. They arrived at 6:30. → You **were cooking** dinner **when** they arrived.
a past action that was ongoing at a specific time	
We **were studying** at 10:30 last night. They **were playing** soccer at 5 o'clock.	It was raining from 10:00 to 10:30. We left at 10:05. → It **was raining when** we left.
questions and negatives	
A: **Were** you **studying**? B: Yes, I **was**. / No, I **wasn't**. I **wasn't studying**. Q: **What was** he **doing**? A: He **was sleeping**.	

> **Brief note**
>
> You can change the order of the two clauses. If the *when* clause comes first, put a comma (,) after the clause.
> **When** they arrived, you **were cooking** dinner.
> **When** we left, it **was raining**.

E Grammar Practice

Fill in the blanks with the correct forms of the verbs. Use the past continuous.

1. We _____ _____ (chat) on the phone all night.

2. They _____ _____ (not watch) TV when I came home.

3. _____ you _____ (work) at 11:00 last night?

4. Olivia _____ _____ (meditate) when the neighbor came over.

5. I _____ _____ (lose) weight last year because I stopped eating fast food.

6. He felt stressed because he _____ _____ (not see) his therapist regularly.

7. _____ the professor _____ (talk) when you left the classroom?

8. How _____ the patient _____ (do) when the doctor saw him?

F Read to Write

Read about Brenda's dream. Underline the past continuous verbs.

In my dream, I was a middle school student again. I was at my school, but the school looked different. I was walking around and looking for my classroom. But I couldn't find it! I was lost, and I was late for class. I was asking other students for help, but they couldn't help. They didn't know, either. I was getting very nervous. Maybe I had this dream because I was worrying about a test all day yesterday. The dream probably means I was feeling stressed about school. Have you ever had a dream like this?

Think about a similar dream you have had, or another dream that was unusual, funny, or scary. On a separate sheet of paper, write a short paragraph about it (five sentences or more). Then read your paragraph to a partner and discuss it.

A   Model Conversation

Read the conversation. Then listen. 🔊 Track 32

Pharmacist: Miss Lopez? Your prescription is ready.

Miss Lopez: Great. How much is it?

Pharmacist: Well, first, we ought to talk about your medication. Did your doctor explain it to you?

Miss Lopez: Yes, it's for the flu.

Pharmacist: That's right. It's effective as a flu treatment if you start taking it soon after the start of symptoms.

Miss Lopez: Well, I started having symptoms this morning.

Pharmacist: Okay. Take one capsule every twelve hours. And be sure to finish the bottle. You might feel better in a couple of days, but you've got to keep taking it.

Miss Lopez: I see. Should I take the capsules with meals?

Pharmacist: You don't have to. But if they cause nausea, you can take them with food. Oh—and if you miss a dose, don't take two capsules the next time. You should always take one at a time.

Miss Lopez: All right. Are there any side effects?

Pharmacist: Nausea is one, as I said. That's no big deal. But if you have trouble breathing or chest pain, call your doctor. This information is on the label, as well.

B   Vocabulary

Write the blue words from the conversation next to the correct definitions.

1. _____ a very small container filled with medicine, which you take like a pill

2. _____ to make (something) happen

3. _____ the amount of medicine you take at one time

4. _____ a piece of paper on something that gives information about it

5. _____ (usually) bad or unwanted things caused by medication

6. _____ a person who works at a pharmacy and is an expert on medications

7. _____ working correctly; having the right effect

8. _____ the front part of the body between the stomach and the neck

9. _____ a way to cure or relieve a medical problem

10. _____ together; at the same time

C   Quick Review

Look back at the brief notes in this module.

1. What preposition do you use to say you are a member of a team?

2. What is the difference in meaning between *workout* and *work out*?

3. What kind of information can you find on a blog?

Grammar

Modals of obligation

Brief note

Of these modals, only *should* and *have to* are commonly used in questions.
Ought to and *have got to* are not commonly used in the negative.

modals of obligation		
You can use a modal + base verb to talk about an obligation. An obligation is something that is necessary.		
weak obligation: advice, suggestions, warnings		
A: **Should** I take the capsules with meals? B: Yes, you **should** take them with meals. You **shouldn't** take them on an empty stomach.	I **ought to** pick up my medicine soon.	She**'d better** remember to take her medicine. She**'d better not** forget.
strong obligation: necessity		
A: **Do** I **have to** go to a pharmacy to buy it? B: Yes, you **have to** go to a pharmacy. But you **don't have to** have a prescription.	You **must** take this medicine every day. You **must not / can't** miss a day.	You **have got to** keep taking it. You**'ve got to** finish the bottle.

Grammar Practice

Listen and circle the correct words. Check your answers with a partner. Then practice reading each sentence aloud. Track 33

1. People (should / have to) not forget to floss.

2. Do you (have got to / have to) take allergy pills every day?

3. That restaurant has delicious food. You (had better / ought to) try it.

4. If you have serious side effects, you (must / can't) call your doctor immediately.

5. (Should / Ought) I take this medicine before bed?

6. I can't buy that medicine yet. (I should / I've got to) get a prescription from a doctor first.

7. I (had better / had better not) go to the pharmacy soon—it closes in an hour.

8. Be sure to finish these capsules. You (must not / don't have to) stop taking them when you feel better.

Use the Language

What should you do about this problem?

Add two more symptoms or illnesses to the list below. Then go online and research what a patient should do about each one. Consider both medicines from a pharmacy and treatments you can do at home. Then compare your list with your partner's. Share your results with the class.

Problem	Treatment
A cold	
A headache	
A sore back	
A runny nose	
A cough	

A Call from the Doctor

Listen to the phone call from Maxim's doctor. Fill in the blanks with the words that you hear. Then listen again and check your answers. `Track 34`

Doctor: Hello, may I speak to Maxim, please? This is Dr. Jasper calling.

Maxim: Hi, Dr. Jasper, it's me.

Doctor: Hi, Maxim. How are you today? Have your _____ changed at all?

Maxim: Well, I've developed a _____ since I saw you. My headache _____ _____ worse as well.

Doctor: Hmm, okay. _____ _____ _____ to come in again as soon as possible. I want you _____ _____ a few tests.

Maxim: Is it serious, doctor?

Doctor: I don't think so. I _____ _____ to a colleague about your case. She seems to think it's an _____. You have a new dog, right?

Maxim: Yes, but I've _____ had an animal allergy before.

Doctor: Getting one at your age is pretty common. I've emailed a _____ to your pharmacy for some medication. It should help with the _____ and the cough. You only _____ _____ take it once a day.

Maxim: Okay. _____ we make an appointment now for those tests?

Doctor: Yes, a patient has _____ _____ his appointment for 9:00 tomorrow morning. Are you free then?

Maxim: Yes, see you then. Thank you for calling.

B Pet Allergies

Go online and find out about pet allergies. What are some common symptoms? What can people do about them? Make some notes.

Notes

With a partner, discuss what you learned. Then imagine you have a new pet, and your roommate or a family member becomes allergic to it. What should you do? Discuss your ideas with the class.

C Reminder

Some Module 2 Goals in Unit 4

Put a check mark (✓) next to the things you can do.

_____ Describe past activities, events, and personal experiences (for example, what you did over the weekend)

_____ Make another person understand the points that are most important to you when you explain something

_____ Make arrangements on the telephone or in person (for example, setting up a medical appointment)

_____ Manage unexpected things that could happen on vacation (for example, needing a dentist)

A Warm Up

With a partner, make a list of possible reasons for seeing a therapist. Brainstorm as many ideas as you can.

_____

_____

_____

B Role-play

Using your ideas from part A, prepare for a role-play. One person will be a therapist, and the other person will be a patient.

Role A: Patient

You are visiting a therapist because (choose a reason from exercise A). You need to explain to the therapist what the problem is. Talk about the history of the situation and how you are feeling about it now. You need to leave the office feeling better about the situation and with some strategies to solve the problem.

Role B: Therapist

You are meeting a new patient who wants to see you because (reason from part A). Listen to what your patient says. Ask questions about the patient's history with the issue. Ask about how the patient is feeling now. Give the patient some strategies to solve his or her problem.

Switch roles and choose another problem from part A.

C Discuss

Use the problem from your role-play as the patient. Describe to a new partner what it was and talk about what the solutions were. Ask for your partner's opinion about it. Does he or she agree or disagree with the solutions? After you have discussed the issue, write a short paragraph (8–10 sentences) about it. Be sure to include any new ideas that you and your new partner had. Share your paragraph with your first partner. What does he or she think of it?

_____

_____

_____

_____

_____

_____

Module ❷ Review

A Vocabulary

Remember and write…

1. …four sports in the Summer Olympics.

   _____ _____ _____ _____

2. …three words or phrases used to make suggestions.

   _____ _____ _____

3. …five body parts people might hurt at the gym.

   _____ _____ _____ _____ _____

B Vocabulary

Match column A with column B to make phrases. Then write the letter of the correct definition next to the new phrase.

A	B	phrase: definition	definition
1. exercise	time	exercise equipment : ___g___	a. pain inside the neck
2. lose	health	_____: _____	b. to clean the mouth with a special liquid
3. get	mouthwash	_____: _____	c. together; at the same time
4. nasty	equipment	_____: _____	d. how good you feel in your mind
5. at a	throat	_____: _____	e. to experience an injury
6. sore	weight	_____: _____	f. to become thinner
7. rinse with	hurt	_____: _____	g. things you use at the gym
8. mental	headache	_____: _____	h. bad pain in the head

C Grammar

Look back at the module. Fill in the blanks.

1. You're sick. You'd _____ stay home today.
2. I _____ like you to _____ this medicine every day.
3. We really enjoy _____ the Olympics on TV.
4. He has studied nutrition _____ two years.
5. It's important _____ you drink water every day.
6. I _____ be starting school next January.
7. She knows _____ to swim really well.
8. They _____ doing homework for hours last night.
9. He recommends _____ I use mouthwash daily.
10. _____ I called, you were talking to your boss.
11. Here, I _____ help you with that.
12. _____ great that you're healthier now.
13. I've known her _____ elementary school.
14. He feels _____ much better now.
15. I _____ to see the doctor yesterday.
16. You have _____ take these pills twice a day.
17. It's not too late. The store hasn't closed _____.
18. She _____ worked at the school for three months.
19. It _____ raining all night.
20. It's fun _____ watch the Olympics.

D Share Ideas

1. Imagine you can add a new sport to the Olympics. It can be one that exists already, or you can create a brand-new sport. What sport will you choose? Discuss with your partner.

2. What do you think is the most common treatment for a cold in your country? Do you have any better ways of treating a cold? What are they? Discuss some ideas with a partner, and then share them with another pair of students.

E Never Ever

In a group, each person says something they have never done before. For example, "I have never ever eaten sushi." The other members of the group give themselves a point if they have done it before. Continue until you are out of ideas. The person with the most points wins the game.

F Describe the Pictures

Write about what you think was happening, has happened, and is happening in each picture. Choose three pictures to talk about with a partner. Be creative! Then share your best ideas with the whole class.

Notes

Healthy Habits

Module 3 Goals

Handle everyday situations such as shopping, making appointments, or checking appointment times

Understand the most important pieces of information in a consumer-related text (for example, price, amount, or nutritional information)

Understand the main points of clear, standard speech on familiar, everyday subjects

Help solve practical problems, saying what you think and asking others what they think

Understand the main points in recorded material about familiar topics

Write short, comprehensible connected texts on familiar subjects

Give practical instructions on how to do something (for example, cooking)

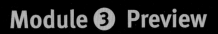

Preview

Look at pages 64 to 89. What pages are these things on?

a steak   _____

a recipe   _____

nail clippers   _____

the passive voice   _____

Discuss

Talk about the questions with a partner.

1. What are the people doing in the photos on the left?

2. What are the names of the foods in the photos on the left?

3. What are some healthy habits?

4. How much money do you spend monthly to look good?

5. How much time do you spend getting ready in the morning?

Write

Choose one of the questions from above. Write a couple of sentences to answer it.

_____

_____

_____

Unit 5

Unit 6

Scan the QR code to watch a preview video.

Lesson 1	The doctor said...

A Model Conversation

Read the conversation. Then listen. 🎧 Track 35

Christa: Hey, how did it go at the clinic?

Adam: Not bad. It's my first checkup since I quit smoking. And I got good news—I'm in pretty good shape. I got a chest X-ray, and my lungs have already started healing.

Christa: That's great! Didn't you only quit two months ago?

Adam: Yeah, your lungs can start healing fast. I also asked for diet advice because I've gained a little weight since quitting. The doctor said to cut down on sugary and alcoholic drinks and to keep walking every day.

Christa: That makes sense. Did she tell you to do anything else?

Adam: Yeah, she actually told me to eat more fat! According to her, I'm eating too much bread and pasta. She said to cut down on those and eat more healthy fats, like fish and salads with olive oil.

Christa: I've heard that, too. They help you lose weight because you feel full for a long time after eating.

Adam: Right. Mmm, now I'm hungry. Let's go get some seafood and salad for lunch.

Brief note

Here, the word "fat" means the oily (liquid or solid) part of certain foods, like butter, nuts, and meat.

B Vocabulary

Listen to the conversation again. Then match the words with the correct definitions. 🎧 Track 35

1. clinic •
2. checkup •
3. diet •
4. lungs •
5. heal •
6. cut down on •
7. sugary •
8. alcoholic •
9. according to •
10. olive oil •

• **a.** an examination by a doctor to check for medical problems
• **b.** to get better after being hurt or damaged
• **c.** having a lot of sugar in it
• **d.** a place to get medical help
• **e.** what a person eats; an eating plan for weight loss, better health, etc.
• **f.** having alcohol in it (for example, beer and wine)
• **g.** a phrase used to say where some information came from
• **h.** liquid fat from olives, which is a common part of Mediterranean diets
• **i.** the part of the body in the chest used for breathing
• **j.** to do or use less of (something)

C In Your World

Do you know anyone who is on a special diet? Who? (It can be you.) Why is this person on this diet? What should and shouldn't he or she eat? Tell a partner.

Should eat	Shouldn't eat

Grammar

Reported speech with infinitives; *about* for topic

reported speech with *said* + (*not*) infinitive / *told* + object + (*not*) infinitive	
original	reported
"You need to get more exercise," the doctor said. "Don't arrive late," said Samantha. "Have another drink," Victor said (to me). "Don't lift too much weight," Gloria said (to her).	The doctor **said to get** more exercise. Samantha **said not to arrive** late. Victor **told me to have** another drink. Gloria **told her not to lift** too much weight.
reported speech with *talked about* / *told* + object + *about* to report the topic of a conversation	
"On our first date, we went to a movie." "I love nightclubs. There are many kinds…"	He **told me about** their first date. She **talked about** nightclubs.

Brief note

The verb *tell* always needs an indirect object that shows who the listener was. The verb *say* cannot have an indirect object in reported instructions, advice, or suggestions.

Grammar Practice

Rewrite the sentences as reported speech. Use the given reporting verbs.

1. "Cut down on fast food," said Dr. Smith. (said)

   _____

2. "You should call the clinic and make an appointment," Karl said to his roommate. (told)

   _____

3. "I'm sorry," said the theater employee, "but you can't bring snacks into the theater." (said)

   _____

4. "I remember the night I met your father," Peter's mom said. "We danced and ate ice cream. We never wanted the night to end." (talked)

   _____

Listen to Write

Listen to a short talk by a nutrition expert. On a separate sheet of paper, take notes on his advice. Compare your notes with a partner's. 🔊 **Track 36**

Now write 4–5 sentences about the talk and the expert's advice.

A   Authentic Text: Health blog

Read the blog post. Then listen. 🔊 Track 37

If you're confused about how to eat right, you're not alone! Everyone recommends that you eat a balanced diet. But there is no *one* way to eat healthily. Everyone needs the same basic nutrients. But your size, physical activity, sex, and age all affect your dietary needs.

1. Size and Physical Activity: If you are tall and exercise a lot, you can eat more and not gain weight. For example, the actor and wrestler Dwayne ("The Rock") Johnson eats 5,000 calories a day. This includes three pounds of fish. But he's 195 centimeters tall and lifts weights six days a week. If your size is average and you don't exercise, you don't need as much food.

2. Sex: Men are bigger than women, so they need to eat more. If you are an active man weighing 175 pounds, you should eat about 2,800 calories a day. If you are an active woman weighing 125 pounds, you should eat about 2,000. Also, men need more protein to avoid losing muscle. Women need more calcium. If they don't get enough, their bones become weak and break more easily.

3. Age: If you're young, your body burns calories quickly. People's ability to burn calories slows down when they get older. It also becomes more difficult for their bodies to get vitamins from food. So if you're over 50, you should eat less, and you might need to take a daily vitamin pill.

B   Vocabulary

Read the blog post again. Then match the words with the correct definitions.

1. calorie •
2. pound •
3. balanced •
4. vitamin •

   • a. having a healthy mix of parts or a fair proportion of parts
   • b. something found naturally in food that is necessary for good health
   • c. a measurement of weight, equal to 0.45 kilogram
   • d. a measurement of the amount of energy in food

Write the letters of the pictures next to the correct words.

5. sex   _____
6. nutrients _____
7. average _____
8. bones _____

   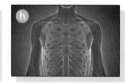

C   Comprehension

Choose the correct answers.

1. What is special about Dwayne Johnson's diet?   a. He eats a lot of calories.   b. He only eats fish.
2. Who should eat more calories, on average?   a. women   b. men   c. older people
3. What do women need more of than men?   a. vitamins   b. protein   c. calcium
4. What do men need more of than women?   a. vitamins   b. protein   c. calcium
5. Who might need to take a daily vitamin pill?   a. young people   b. women   c. older people

D   In Your World

Make a list of foods you usually eat. Discuss your list with a partner. Which foods do you think are healthy and unhealthy? How does eating these foods make you feel?

Grammar

Zero conditional

Zero conditional sentences are *if* sentences about general facts in the present. Both clauses are in the simple present. The result clause may or may not begin with *then*.

	condition	result	
If	you **exercise** a lot, you**'re** young, they **have** a big lunch, people **don't eat**,	(then) you **can eat** more. (then) your body **burns** calories quickly. (then) they **feel** tired in the afternoon. (then) they **get** hungry.	**Brief note** You can switch the order of the clauses: *Your body burns calories quickly if you're young.*

Grammar Practice

Put the words in order to make sentences. Try writing the sentences again with the clauses in a different order.

1. feel / if / fat / eat / you / you / full

   _____.

2. unhealthy / weight / too / if / gain / you / become / you / much

   _____.

3. I / healthy / eat / plenty / have / if / energy / of / I / food

   _____.

4. weak / if / don't / bones / women's / they / calcium / eat / become

   _____.

Use the Language

Travel advice

Work in small groups. Imagine a traveler is coming from a foreign country. Discuss what advice you would give him or her about eating and drinking in your country. Write your advice in complete sentences and share it with other groups. Are your lists similar or different? In what ways?

_____

_____

_____

_____

A Model Conversation

Read the conversation. Then listen. Track 38

Brief note

A "vegetarian" is a person who does not eat any meat. *Vegetarian* can also be an adjective: *vegetarian recipes.*

Mike: Hey, Julia, would you like a **steak**? They're almost ready.

Julia: Actually, I brought some vegetables to grill. I'm a vegetarian.

Mike: Really? Wow. Was it hard to stop eating meat?

Julia: It was at first, but it's been two years, and I've never felt better.

Mike: That's good, but I read an article recently. It said that people need meat to get enough protein and a certain vitamin. I forget which one.

Julia: It's vitamin B12. Well, there's protein in eggs and **beans**, so I eat those a lot. And eggs have vitamin B12, too.

Mike: I see. Why did you stop eating meat, if you don't mind my asking?

Julia: At first, it was for weight loss. Then my doctor told me vegetarians have less **risk** of heart **disease** and **cancer**.

Mike: Well, I still can't live without meat. Steak is so delicious, and vegetables are so **bland**.

Julia: They're not if you know how to cook them! You just need the right **spices** and **recipes**.

B Vocabulary

Listen to the conversation again. Then fill in the blanks with the bold words from the conversation. Track 38

1. My mom keeps all her favorite _____ in a box in the kitchen.

2. If you don't brush your teeth twice a day, you have a higher _____ of cavities.

3. I'd like to order the grilled _____, but it's so expensive. I'd better get the chicken.

4. Chili and cinnamon are common _____ that are used in everyday cooking.

5. People often eat _____ with rice.

6. If you have nausea or a stomachache, you should only eat _____ foods.

7. Smoking is dangerous. Smokers have a high risk of getting lung _____.

8. Cancer is a serious _____. Millions of people die from it each year.

C In Your World

Work with a partner. Make a list of foods that have lots of protein, a list of bland foods, and a list of any vitamins and other nutrients that you know. Compare your list with another pair's. Discuss the differences.

Foods with Protein	Bland Foods	Vitamins and Other Nutrients

D Grammar

Reported speech with *that* clauses

To report past statements that are still true, use a past tense reporting verb (for example, *said*) with a simple present verb in the reported speech: subject + *said* (*that*) + clause; subject + *told* + object + (*that*) + clause

original	reported
"Vegetables are so bland," he said.	He **said that** vegetables are bland.
"You shouldn't eat before dinner," Mom said (to me).	Mom **told me that** I shouldn't eat before dinner.
"Vegetarians have a lower risk of developing cancer," the doctor said (to me).	The doctor **told me** vegetarians have a lower risk of developing cancer.

Brief note

In conversation, the word *that* can be left out: *He said vegetables are bland.*

E Grammar Practice

In each reported past statement, one word is missing or incorrect. Underline the mistake. Then write the correct word or the missing word.

1. The doctor said me that I should eat more vegetables. _____

2. She saying that you don't get enough vitamin C. _____

3. I told he shouldn't drink so much alcohol. _____

4. The article said that there was protein in beans. _____

5. Yesterday Sam tells me my diet isn't healthy. _____

Rewrite each sentence as reported speech.

6. "There are great recipes online," he said.

    _____

7. "Eggs have important nutrients," the professor said to us.

    _____

8. "It's not hard to eat a vegetarian diet," the doctor said to me.

    _____

F Use the Language

Where should we eat?

Go online and look up reviews of nearby restaurants. Find one that you like or would like to try. Then write four sentences reporting what you read.

1.
2.
3.
4.

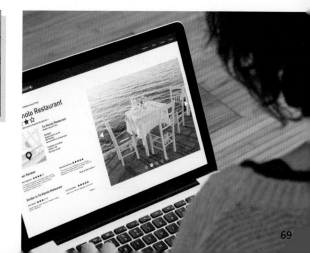

Now get in groups and decide where your group will eat tonight. Try to convince your partners that your place is the best based on your research.

A Model Conversation

Read the conversation. Then listen. 🔊 Track 39

Nutrition Facts

Serving Size	52 g

Amount Per Serving		
Calories 150	Calories from Fat	45

	% Daily Value*
Total Fat 5 g	8%
Saturated Fat 5 g	8%
Trans Fat 0 g	0%
Cholesterol 0 mg	0%
Sodium 100 mg	4%
Total Carbohydrate 38 g	13%
Dietary Fiber less than 1 g	3%
Sugars 17 g	
Protein 2 g	

Vitamin A 0% • Vitamin C 0% • Calcium 0% • Iron 4%

INGREDIENTS: WHOLE GRAIN WHEAT, SUGAR, RICE, WHEAT BRAN, BROWN SUGAR SYRUP, SOLUBLE WHEAT FIBER, CONTAINS 2% OR LESS OF SALT, MALT FLAVORING, STRAWBERRY FLAVORING

Marta: We need breakfast food. Ooh, this cereal looks good.

Jill: Strawberry Crunch? Let me see the box. Craig, my personal trainer, says people should read the label on everything. Oh, look at the ingredients: wheat, sugar—sugar is second!

Marta: A little sugar isn't so bad. It only has 150 calories per serving. Plus, I love strawberries.

Jill: But this cereal doesn't have real strawberries, just strawberry flavor. And it's not nutritious at all. See? The label says there are no vitamins, no calcium...

Marta: Okay, put it back. What do you suggest we get for breakfast?

Jill: Let's get some fresh strawberries, or frozen ones. And some yogurt. We can put them in the blender and make smoothies.

Marta: Okay, but there's yogurt in our fridge already. By the way, what does Craig say about frozen fruits?

Jill: He tells me they're usually as nutritious as fresh ones.

> **Brief note**
> A "smoothie" is a fruit drink made by mixing the ingredients in a blender.

B Vocabulary

Listen to the conversation again. Choose the correct answers. 🔊 Track 39

1. An **ingredient** is _____.
   a. a type of prepared food   b. one part of a prepared food
2. A **frozen** food is _____.
   a. very cold   b. very bland
3. A **serving** of a food is _____.
   a. the amount you buy   b. the amount to eat at one time
4. **Nutritious** foods are _____.
   a. healthy   b. expensive

Match the words with the correct pictures.

5. wheat _____
6. yogurt _____
7. blender _____
8. fridge _____

 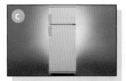 

C In Your World

Work with a partner. Look at the foods below. Make guesses about their nutrition facts. Then find real nutrition labels for these foods online. How close were your guesses? Compare with another pair of students.

pancakes

Ingredients: _____

Calories per serving: _____

Sugar per serving: ____ g (grams)

vanilla ice cream

Ingredients: _____

Calories per serving: _____

Fat per serving: ____ g (grams)

Grammar

Reported speech with simple present tense

Use a reporting verb in the simple present to report things that people have often said, opinions that people still hold, and things that are currently written on signs, labels, etc.: subject + *say/says* (*that*) + clause; subject + *tell/tells* + object + (*that*) + clause	
original	reported
"Yogurt is good for breakfast," she says to me.	She **tells me (that)** yogurt is good for breakfast.
"People should read labels," Craig often says.	Craig often **says (that)** people should read labels.
Calcium 0%	The label **says (that)** there's no calcium.

Grammar Practice

Rewrite the sentences as reported speech. Use the correct form of the verbs in the simple present.

1. Fresh fruit is too expensive, according to Alan. (say)

   _____

2. "Athletes need to drink lots of water," Dr. Garcia often says to his patients. (tell)

   _____

3. You can't park here, according to the sign. (say)

   _____

4. "Many women don't get enough vitamin D," Isabella says to me. (tell)

   _____

5. "Fruit juice can have as much sugar in it as soda," Franklin often explains to his kids. (tell)

   _____

Read to Speak

Work with a partner. Each of you read one of the paragraphs below. Tell each other what you read.

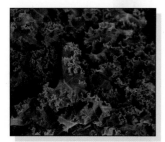

Kale, sometimes called "the king of green vegetables," is one of the healthiest foods in the world. One cup of kale contains 14 important vitamins and nutrients. Eating kale is a fantastic way to increase the amount of nutrients in your diet. Kale has lots of vitamin C. This vitamin helps our bodies fight many diseases. Kale also has several nutrients that help prevent cancer and heart disease. It has nutrients that can help you lose weight, see better, and live longer, too. So add some kale to your diet today. You'll be glad you did!

Acai is a berry found in the rainforests of the Amazon. It is often praised for its health benefits. Acai is high in vitamin C, which boosts a person's immune system and even helps prevent cancer. Some people think acai berries help them lose weight. People who regularly have a handful of acai berries also think it decreases exhaustion and gives them more energy throughout the day.

Lesson 5 — If you cook them too long...

A Authentic Text: Recipe

Read the recipe.

Chicken with Broccoli and Red Pepper

Ingredients: 1 pound of chicken, 2 cups of rice, 1 cup of broccoli, 1 red pepper, 2 tablespoons of soy sauce, 2 tablespoons of olive oil

Directions:

1. Combine the rice with 4 cups of water in a saucepan. If you use less water, you will have drier rice. Put the saucepan on the stove on high heat. When the water is boiling, reduce the heat and let it cook for 20 minutes.
2. Chop the chicken and vegetables into small pieces. Stir-fry them with the olive oil and then quickly remove them from the stove. Check that the chicken is cooked through and not raw on the inside. Be careful, though. If you cook them too long, they will burn.
3. When the rice is cooked, combine it with the chicken and vegetables. Add seasoning and soy sauce. Enjoy this healthy dish!

> **Brief note**
> Sometimes the "directions" in a recipe are called the method.

B Vocabulary

Read the recipe again. Match each word with a picture.

1. cup _____
2. broccoli _____
3. pepper _____
4. tablespoon _____
5. saucepan _____

a  b   c   d   e

C Vocabulary: Cooking

Match the words with the correct definitions.

1. combine •
2. reduce •
3. seasoning •
4. raw •
5. remove •

- a. to make lower
- b. uncooked
- c. to put together
- d. to take away; to take off
- e. something (such as salt, spices, or herbs) that is added to improve the taste of food

D About You

Tell a partner how to make a dish you know how to cook. As you talk, your partner writes the recipe. Then switch roles.

Name of dish: _____

Ingredients: _____

_____

Directions: _____

_____

E Grammar

First conditional

First conditional sentences are *if* sentences about the future. The *if* clause is in the simple present, and the result clause is in the future tense with *will/won't*. The result clause may or may not begin with *then*.

	condition	result	
If	you **don't eat** enough nutrients, you **cook** the vegetables too long, we **eat** a lot of broccoli, I **keep** lifting weights,	(then) you **will get** sick. (then) they **will burn**. (then) we**'ll get** enough vitamin C. (then) I **won't be** weak.	

Brief note

You can switch the order of the clauses:
I won't be weak if I keep lifting weights.

F Grammar Practice

Fill in the blanks with your own ideas to make true first conditional sentences.

1. If I am late for my next class, _____.

2. _____, I won't have much energy.

3. If you don't eat enough protein, _____.

4. _____, you'll gain weight.

5. If you start cooking all your meals at home, _____.

6. _____ if I never eat meat again.

7. If you eat at fast-food restaurants often, _____.

8. _____, you will get sick.

G Use the Language

If you eat our product…

Work in small groups. Create an advertisement for a food or drink. It can be a real food or drink or your own idea. Include some information about its ingredients, instructions for preparing it, and its effects on people's health.

Now take turns "selling" your product to the rest of the class.

A These are healthy cookies!

Listen to a conversation at a supermarket. Fill in the blanks with the words that you hear. Then answer the questions. 🔊 Track 40

Susie: Let's see. We have vegetables, chicken, fish, _____ _____... What else do we need?

Lucas: How about these cookies? Just a small box.

Susie: We really shouldn't, Lucas. The doctor said _____ _____ eating sweet snacks, remember?

Lucas: Yeah, but these are *healthy* cookies! The _____ _____ they don't have much fat and only 100 _____ per serving.

Susie: What's the first _____ on the list?

Lucas: Well, it's sugar.

Susie: See? We've worked so hard to lose weight and get _____ _____. If we start buying cookies, _____ go back to our bad old _____.

Lucas: You're right. We'd better not.

Susie: Don't look so sad. I know you miss _____, but we can get something tasty to cook for dinner. My sister gave me a _____ for Mexican rice and _____. She said it's _____.

Lucas: Okay, where are the beans?

1. What does Lucas want to buy? _____

2. What did their doctor tell them? _____

3. What did Susie's sister say about the recipe for rice and beans? _____

_____

B Role-play

Pretend to shop for food with a partner. Find a grocery advertisement on your phone or in a newspaper. Use language from the unit to discuss what to buy and what not to buy. List the foods below.

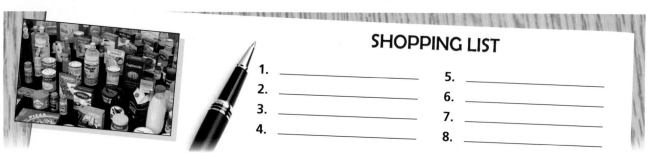

SHOPPING LIST

1. _____   5. _____
2. _____   6. _____
3. _____   7. _____
4. _____   8. _____

C Reminder

Some Module 3 Goals in Unit 5

Put a check mark (✓) next to the things you can do.

_____ Understand the main points of clear, standard speech on familiar, everyday subjects

_____ Handle everyday situations such as shopping, making appointments, or checking appointment times

_____ Give practical instructions on how to do something (for example, cooking)

74

Read to Write

Read part of a talk about nutrition. Then circle the correct words and fill in the blanks to complete the sentences.

"People get most of their protein from meat and cheese. Every person needs a different amount of protein each day. Young children need less protein, and people who work out and play sports need more. But everyone needs protein. Without it, you won't have strong bones and muscles."

Rebecca Beare, M.D.

1. The doctor (said / told) that every person _____ a different amount of protein.

2. According to the doctor, if people (won't / don't) get enough protein, _____
_____.

Speak to Write

Work with a partner. Practice saying the sentences below, taking turns filling in the blanks with your own words. How many different ways can you think of to complete each sentence?

1. He needs to stop smoking. If he doesn't quit, _____.

2. If you always eat at restaurants, _____.

3. My doctor tells me that _____.

Now Write

Read the paragraph. Then write a summary (a statement of the most important information) in your own words in ten minutes or less.

Making small changes in your diet can make a big difference. Experts on nutrition advise people to fill half of their plates at each meal with fruits and vegetables. That's a good way to start. People should also eat less salt and sugar because they increase the risk of heart disease and other illnesses. To begin cutting down on unhealthy snacks, drink one less soda and eat one less sweet or salty snack each day. Learning to eat healthily is like learning to walk. If you take one small step at a time, you'll soon be running!

_____

_____

_____

_____

Lesson 1   Getting Ready in the Morning

A   Model Conversation

Read the conversation. Then listen. 🔘 Track 41

Tom: Will you be in the bathroom much longer, Ray? I need the mirror.

Ray: A little bit longer. I just finished shaving, and I need to shower before my lunch date. I'll be quick—I don't even need to shampoo.

Tom: I'm trying to be patient, but you know I have a job interview in 45 minutes, right? I've got to shave.

Ray: Oh, I forgot about that. Well, you need to put on your suit, don't you? Why don't you go do that, and comb your hair? I'll be out of the shower when you're done.

Tom: No, I might get shaving cream on my suit.

Ray: All right, you go first. You know, my brother and his roommates made a bathroom schedule, so they never have arguments like this.

Tom: Thanks, Ray. We should probably do that, too.

B   Vocabulary

Listen to the words. Then match each word with the correct picture. 🔘 Track 42

comb	shave	mirror	cream	suit

_____   _____   _____   _____   _____

Match each word with the correct definition.

1. patient   •   •   **a.** to wash your hair; special soap used to wash hair
2. argument   •   •   **b.** able to wait and not become angry
3. shampoo   •   •   **c.** to dress yourself in (clothes)
4. put on   •   •   **d.** a fight in words; a disagreement

C   About You

Think of five things you do to get ready every morning. Write them in the order that you do them. Then compare your list with a partner's.

1. _____   3. _____   5. _____

2. _____   4. _____

D Grammar

Tag questions

<table>
<tr><td colspan="3" align="center">tag questions</td></tr>
<tr><td colspan="3">Tag questions are added at the end of statements. They are used when the speaker expects a certain answer and just wants to make sure. Positive statements are followed by negative tag questions, and negative statements are followed by positive tag questions.

The form of a tag question is auxiliary verb (+ not) + subject? (Auxiliary verbs include be, do, have, and modals.) Contractions are almost always used.</td></tr>
<tr><td>positive statement</td><td>negative tag question</td><td>expected answer</td></tr>
<tr><td>We need to buy some shampoo,</td><td>don't we?</td><td>Yes, we do.</td></tr>
<tr><td>You're wearing a new suit,</td><td>aren't you?</td><td>Yes, I am.</td></tr>
<tr><td>I took a long shower,</td><td>didn't I?</td><td>Yes, you did.</td></tr>
<tr><td>negative statement</td><td>positive tag question</td><td>expected answer</td></tr>
<tr><td>He never combs his hair,</td><td>does he?</td><td>No, he doesn't.</td></tr>
<tr><td>You won't be late,</td><td>will you?</td><td>No, I won't.</td></tr>
<tr><td>You haven't shaved yet,</td><td>have you?</td><td>No, I haven't.</td></tr>
</table>

Brief note

The words *right* and *huh* are often used in the same way as tag questions. (*Huh* is very informal.) They can follow either positive or negative statements.
*We need to buy some shampoo, **right**?*
*You haven't shaved yet, **huh**?*

E Grammar Practice

Circle the correct answers.

1. You have a bath every morning, (don't you / you don't)?　　(Yes / No), I do.
2. Mike didn't wash his hands before lunch, (did he / was he)?　　(Yes / No), he didn't.
3. You'll get ready fast, (won't you / will you)?　　(Yes / No), I will.
4. You haven't used my face cream, (did you / have you)?　　(Yes / No), I have. Sorry!
5. Kelly should wear a suit, (should she / shouldn't she)?　　(Yes / No), that's not necessary.
6. This is your comb, (right / is it)?　　(Yes / No), it's Jim's.

F Use the Language

Survey on bathroom products

1. Imagine you work for a company that makes toothpaste, shaving cream, and other bathroom products. You are going to interview people about their morning routines. Make a list of questions you can ask. Ask three classmates the questions and make notes on their answers.

Questions	Person 1	Person 2	Person 3
1.			
2.			
3.			
4.			
5.			

2. Look at the results. Find the most common and the most interesting answers. Present your findings to the class.

A   Model Conversation

Brief note
The word "soap" means something that is used for washing. It can be solid or liquid.

Read the conversation. Then listen. Track 43

Frank: Do you need some help choosing a cleanser?

Donna: Yes, actually. My **skin** is **oily**, and I have a little **acne**, too. What's good for that?

Frank: This one is great. I use it, and my skin is clear now. It's very **gentle** on your skin and better than regular soap.

Donna: Sounds good. Thanks for your help!

Frank: Wouldn't you like to get some moisturizer, too? The cleanser works great, but it can dry your skin.

Donna: Oh. But don't face lotions make acne worse?

Frank: Some do, but not this one. It also has sunscreen.

Donna: Hmm, okay. That reminds me—I need sunscreen for my body, too.

Frank: Those are right over here. I recommend this brand, Summer Sport. Even if you **sweat** a lot or go swimming, it'll still work.

Brief note
A "brand" is a specific kind of product from a specific company. A "product" is any item that a company makes and sells.

Donna: All right, I'll take it.

Frank: Can I show you some makeup as well?

Donna: Thanks, but I think I'm buying enough skin products for today!

B   Vocabulary

Fill in the blanks with the correct bold words from the conversation.

1. If you wash your face too often, your _____ will get dry.

2. Do you _____ a lot when you work out?

3. This soap is good because it is _____ on your skin.

4. It's very common to get _____ when you are a teenager.

5. People often have _____ skin on their noses.

Match each word with the correct definition.

6. cleanser •   • **a.** a cream or lotion that protects your skin from the sun

7. lotion •   • **b.** a liquid-like product that you rub onto your skin without rinsing it off

8. sunscreen •   • **c.** a product that you put on your face to look better; cosmetic

9. makeup •   • **d.** a product that is used for washing the skin that is not soap

C   About You

You are going on a one-week trip to a place with no stores nearby. List all the toiletries you will need to pack. (Toiletries are the things you keep in the bathroom for cleaning yourself and for skin care.) Use a dictionary if necessary.

Now imagine you can only take two of the above products. Which would you choose? Circle them. Discuss your choices and your reasons with a partner.

D Grammar

Negative questions

negative questions	
Like negative tag questions, negative questions are used when speakers expect the answer to be yes. These questions are also a way to express surprise at unexpected news and to ask about it. *A: I'd better be going.* *B: Already? Aren't you staying for dinner?*	

negative question	expected answer
Don't you wear makeup?	Yes, I do.
Shouldn't he use sunscreen?	Yes, he should.
Isn't this good for oily skin?	Yes, it is.
Wouldn't you like some moisturizer, too?	Yes, I would.

Brief note

Even though these questions have the word *not* in them, you answer them in the same way as regular questions.

A: Do you wear makeup?
B: Yes. All the time. / No, I don't.
A: Don't you wear makeup?
B: Yes. All the time. / No, I don't.

E Grammar Practice

Fill in the blanks to make negative questions.

1. Q: _____ this store sell makeup?

   A: No, it doesn't. It only sells medicine.

2. Q: _____ you try some of this sunscreen?

   A: Yes, I think I will.

3. Q: _____ you want to borrow my mirror?

   A: Yes, I do.

4. Q: _____ this lotion only for women?

   A: No, men use it, too.

5. Q: _____ these products expensive?

   A: Yes, but they work well and smell nice.

6. Q: _____ you shopped here before?

   A: Yeah, I've shopped here many times.

F Use the Language

New skin products

1. With a partner, you are going to create a new brand of soap, sunscreen, or makeup (choose one). Think about how people can use it, how it's different, and why people will like it. Choose a name for your product. Write down your ideas.

   Name of product: _____

   Type of product: _____

   Notes about the product:

2. Talk to another pair of students. Ask them questions about their new product. Explain your product to them.

A Model Monologue

Read the monologue. Then listen. 🎧 Track 44

Brief note

A (hair) "salon" is a place people go to have their hair cut, dyed, or styled. The people who work there are called "hairstylists". People who mostly do simple haircuts for men are called *barbers*.

William: At my high school, there were a lot of rules about how students had to look. There were even rules about our hair! We couldn't dye our hair or shave our heads. Boys' hair had to be short and neat, and we couldn't have any facial hair. We all looked so similar.

Now I'm in college, and I don't have to follow these rules anymore. I'm letting my hair grow for the first time. It's spiky right now, but I'm going to let it grow to shoulder-length. Then I'll wear it in a ponytail. My natural color is red, but I'm going to the hairstylist to dye it a different color. I'd rather not go to a

salon, but I don't want to mess it up by doing it myself. I also haven't decided if I want to dye it blue or black. I hope the hairstylist can help me decide.

Alec has dyed black hair and a mohawk. (His hair is shaved on the sides and stands up straight on top.) People sometimes stare at him, but I think it looks cool. Rules are fine for kids, but adults should be creative with their hairstyles. It's a fun way to stand out from the crowd.

Brief note

"Stand out from the crowd" means to look or be different from other people (usually in a positive way).

B Vocabulary

Match each word or phrase with the correct picture. Then listen to the monologue again and circle the words or phrases the man mentions. 🎧 Track 44

a. ponytail	**b.** bald	**c.** bangs	**d.** hairstylist/hairdresser
e. dyed hair	**f.** short, spiky hair	**g.** shoulder-length hair	**h.** perm

1. _____

3. _____

5. _____

7. _____

2. _____

4. _____

6. _____

8. _____

C In Your World

What did your hair look like three years ago? What did it look like when you were in elementary school? Tell a partner. Report your partner's descriptions to the class.

Grammar

Content clauses with *if* and *whether*

> **Brief note**
>
> The subject and verb switch positions in direct questions but not in content clauses.

content clauses with *if* and *whether*	

Yes/No questions can be made into content clauses beginning with *if* or *whether*. They have the form *if/whether* + subject + verb phrase.

These clauses often follow verbs such as *know, remember, decide, ask, check,* etc. These clauses may or may not end with *or not*.

Questions giving two choices (with *or*) can also be made into *if/whether* content clauses. These clauses do not end with *or not*.

direct question	statement with content clause
Does she have a perm?	We can't remember **if/whether** she has a perm (or not).
Did he cut his hair?	Ask him **if/whether** he cut his hair (or not).
Should I dye my hair blue or black?	I haven't decided **if/whether** I should dye my hair blue **or** black.
Is that a barbershop or a salon?	I don't know **if/whether** that's a barbershop **or** a salon.

Grammar Practice

Put the words in order to make sentences.

1. she / hairstylist / I'll / her / if / knows / ask / a

   _____.

2. with / the / ponytail / is / Ginny / I / wonder / if / the / girl

   _____.

3. is / open / or / not / please / hair / whether / the / check / salon

   _____.

4. decided / hasn't / whether / wants / he / or / long / hair / short / he

   _____.

5. remember / she / if / doesn't / straight / was / my / or / hair / curly

   _____.

Use the Language

Interesting hairstyles

1. Think of the last time you changed your hairstyle. Write the conversation you had with your hairstylist. Then with a partner, role-play your conversation. Switch roles, and practice again.

2. Find some magazines with plenty of photos of people or search online for celebrity hairstyles. With a partner, find four images of interesting hairstyles that you both like. Show your images to another pair of students. Let them see them for only five seconds. Then hide the images.

   The other pair must try and remember the styles they saw. Then they must describe each image to you and your partner. If they get it right, give them the image. Switch roles and describe their images. The team with the most correct descriptions wins the game!

A   Authentic Text: Magazine article

Read the article.

Your Nails, Your Health   by Dr. Ahmed Kaya, M.D.

Many people don't care about how their nails look. True, no one needs to pay for professional manicures or pedicures. But nail care is part of good hygiene and grooming. And did you know that it can even affect your health? Here's what both men and women should do to care for their nails.

1. Watch the color of your nails.

Smoking or using dark **nail polish** can cause nails to turn yellow. This usually isn't a reason to worry. But dark spots can be a symptom of skin cancer, so if you see them, contact a doctor immediately.

2. Keep your nails clean, and clip or file them often.

Dirty nails can cause infections. So can broken ones, since they can cause tears in the skin. Wash your hands often and brush dirty nails with a clean toothbrush. Use **clippers** or a **nail file** regularly to keep the ends smooth. Do this for both your **fingernails** and your **toenails**.

3. Don't bite your nails.

Biting your nails also brings a risk of infection in both your fingers and mouth. First, try to understand why and when you bite your nails. Usually, it's stress. Learn to relieve stress in other ways. There are also special nail polishes that taste bad to help you stop biting.

> **Brief note**
>
> "Hygiene" is what people do to keep their bodies clean. "Grooming" is what people do to look nice. For example, washing your hair is hygiene, and combing it is grooming.

B   Vocabulary

Write each bold word from the article under the correct picture.

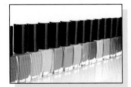    

_____   _____   _____   _____   _____

Match each word with the correct definition.

1. manicure •
2. pedicure •
3. affect •
4. infection •

   • **a.** to change or have an effect on someone or something
   • **b.** a treatment to improve the looks and health of the hands and fingernails
   • **c.** a disease caused by germs (very small living things) entering the body
   • **d.** a treatment to improve the looks and health of the feet and toenails

C   Vocabulary Comprehension

Fill in the blanks with the correct words from part B.

1. My feet look terrible. I should give myself a(n) _____.

2. It's easy to know when Jack is nervous because he bites his _____.

3. Wendy works a lot with her hands, so she doesn't get _____ or wear _____.

4. If you cut yourself, wash the cut with soap and water to prevent a(n) _____.

5. You can use a(n) _____ to make the edges of your nails round.

6. Everyone knows that people's mental health can _____ their physical health.

7. I need to cut my fingernails, but I can't find my _____. Can I borrow yours?

D Grammar

Content clauses with *wh-* questions

Brief note

As in content clauses with *if* and *whether*, the subject comes before the verb.

content clauses with *wh-* questions	
Like yes/no questions, *wh-* questions can become content clauses in statements. The form is *wh-* word/phrase + subject + verb phrase.	
These content clauses follow many of the same verbs as *if/whether* clauses. (See lesson 3.)	

wh- question	statement with content clause
What style of manicure would you like?	I don't know **what style of manicure** you would like.
Where did you buy that nail polish?	She asked **where** I bought that nail polish.
How long will the appointment be?	He's checking **how long** the appointment will be.
When can we go for a pedicure?	She'll decide **when** we can go for a pedicure.

E Grammar Practice

Complete the sentences with content clauses. Use the correct pronouns where necessary.

1. "Where are my nail clippers?" asked John.

   → John's asking _____.

2. "Why do people get pedicures?" asked Maya.

   → Maya wants to know _____.

3. "Which color will look better on my nails?" she asked.

   → She can't decide _____.

4. "How much does a manicure cost?" I asked.

   → Please check _____.

5. "Who is working at the nail salon today?" Kim asked.

   → Kim doesn't know _____.

F Use the Language

Beauty businesses

1. Work with a partner. People go to many kinds of businesses to improve their appearance. Hair salons and nail salons are two examples. List three more. Note some of the products and services people get at each place.

Hair salons	Nail salons	_____	_____	_____

2. Get in groups. Discuss the businesses you listed above. Which are the most popular in your area? Why? Which of them do you use? Are there any that you don't and never will use? Why?

3. Which answers above did you and your partners agree on? Tell the rest of the class.

A   Authentic Text: Brochure

Read the brochure. Then listen. 🔊 **Track 45**

Brief note
A "coconut" is a fruit that grows in hot places and is white on the inside.

Special Deal for First-Time Visitors to *New You Spa*: Coconut Massage

If you've never been to our **spa** before, now is the time. All new customers are given a 25% **discount** on our full-body coconut **massage**! All your needs are taken care of by our experienced massage therapists. With our coconut massage:

- You are **covered** in **soothing** coconut oil—every part of your skin.
- You are massaged from head to toe.
- You are **scrubbed** with coconut husk (the outer part of the fruit)—removing all the dead, dry skin.
- You are **bathed** in coconut milk while you are served coconut milk tea—feel all your stress **disappear**!

Make a reservation now for your massage, or consider booking a full weekend to enjoy our **luxurious accommodations**.

Come to New You Spa and pamper yourself today!
Visit us at thenewyou.com/booking.

Brief note
To "pamper" means to treat extremely well; to take very good care of.

B   Vocabulary

Write the bold words and phrases from part A next to the correct definitions.

1. _____ the action of rubbing or pressing someone's body to help relax the muscles or to relieve pain
2. _____ placed into a liquid
3. _____ rich; stylish; very comfortable
4. _____ rubbed back and forth on the skin roughly
5. _____ a place people go to improve their appearance and health by relaxing, getting skin treatments, etc.
6. _____ a special, lower price
7. _____ relaxing; calming
8. _____ to go away; to no longer exist or be present
9. _____ a place where a visitor can sleep and get other services
10. _____ spread over with something

C   Quick Review

Look back at the grammar tables in this module. Match each grammar point on the left with the correct example on the right.

1. zero conditional •   • a. Clara asked how much the capsules cost.
2. tag question •   • b. He told me he has a cold.
3. reported speech •   • c. Your salon does pedicures, doesn't it?
4. first conditional •   • d. If people don't brush their teeth, they get cavities.
5. content clause •   • e. If you bite your nails, they'll look terrible.

D Grammar

Passive voice

Brief note

The phrase *by* + (doer of the action) is optional. It can be included or left out, depending on how important it is to the meaning.

passive voice
Most sentences are in the active voice. This means the subject is the doer of the action: *The spa offers massages.*
When the doer of an action is unknown or is less important, we use the passive voice. In the passive voice, the subject receives the action: *Massages **are offered** (by the spa).*
The form of the passive is *be* + past participle. The verb *be* shows the tense. Passive verbs can be in any tense.

active	passive
We **give** a discount.	A discount **is given** (by us).
The spa's employees **pamper** you.	You **are pampered** (by the spa's employees).
I **scrubbed** my hands at the sink.	My hands **were scrubbed** at the sink (by me).
The hairstylist **didn't dye** his hair.	His hair **wasn't dyed** (by the hairstylist).
Did they **make** the reservations?	**Were** the reservations **made** (by them)?

E Grammar Practice

Circle the correct answers.

1. The baby (was / has) bathed by her parents.

2. The coconut oil (has / is) rubbed into the skin.

3. Manicures aren't (gave / given) at this spa.

4. Was our room (cleaning / cleaned)?

Fill in the blanks using the correct passive forms of the verbs.

5. This brand of coconut milk is delicious. It _____ (make) in Thailand.

6. A massage _____ (book) by the woman yesterday.

7. My favorite face lotion _____ (not sell) in any stores these days.

8. In a hot-stone massage, hot stones _____ (put) on a person's back.

9. _____ your bill at the spa _____ (pay) by your parents?

F Use the Language

Perfect spa experience

Look at the brochure in part A again. Think about other services offered at spas. Do online research if necessary. Write down your own ideas for the perfect spa experience.

Then talk to a partner. Exchange ideas and take notes. What ideas do you agree and disagree about?

My perfect spa experience	My partner's perfect spa experience

A Making an Appointment

Listen to a woman making an appointment at a salon. Fill in the blanks with the words from the box. Then listen again and check your answers. ● Track 46

| you'll | if | are painted | don't you | how long | right |
| haven't | he starts | nail polish | hairstylist | manicure | discount |

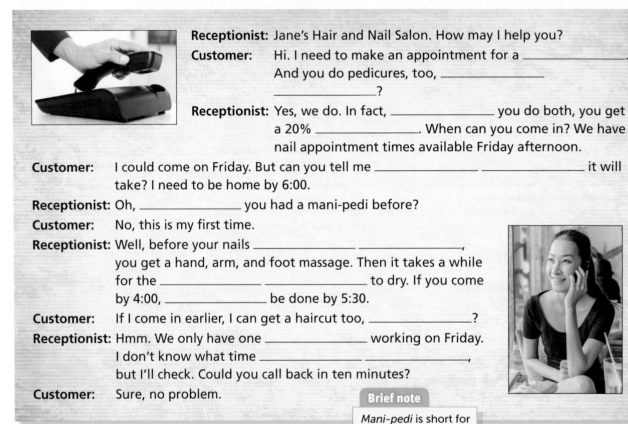

Receptionist: Jane's Hair and Nail Salon. How may I help you?

Customer: Hi. I need to make an appointment for a _____. And you do pedicures, too, _____ _____?

Receptionist: Yes, we do. In fact, _____ you do both, you get a 20% _____. When can you come in? We have nail appointment times available Friday afternoon.

Customer: I could come on Friday. But can you tell me _____ _____ it will take? I need to be home by 6:00.

Receptionist: Oh, _____ you had a mani-pedi before?

Customer: No, this is my first time.

Receptionist: Well, before your nails _____ _____, you get a hand, arm, and foot massage. Then it takes a while for the _____ _____ to dry. If you come by 4:00, _____ be done by 5:30.

Customer: If I come in earlier, I can get a haircut too, _____?

Receptionist: Hmm. We only have one _____ working on Friday. I don't know what time _____ _____, but I'll check. Could you call back in ten minutes?

Customer: Sure, no problem.

> **Brief note**
>
> *Mani-pedi* is short for manicure-pedicure.

B Make the Call

With a partner, go online and research a hair salon, nail salon, or spa nearby. Then create a conversation like the one above. Include the following information:

- the name of the business
- the services and/or products the customer wants
- the services and/or products the shop offers
- the day and time of the appointment

C Reminder

Some Module 3 Goals in Unit 6

Put a check mark (✓) next to the things you can do.

_____ Understand the most important pieces of information in a consumer-related text (for example, price, amount, or nutritional information)

_____ Help solve practical problems, saying what you think and asking others what they think

_____ Write short, comprehensible connected texts on familiar subjects

Warm Up

Work with a partner. Cover the rest of the page below. How many vocabulary words related to skin, hair, and nails can you remember in five minutes? Write them in the correct boxes.

skin	hair	nails
	comb	

Read for Information

Read the blog post and the comments from readers below. Then answer the questions.

Classy Men

A stylish man…

1. cuts his nails with nail clippers once a week and never bites his nails.
2. knows a good barber and sees him or her regularly. He knows what hairstyle looks good on him, and his hair is never longer than shoulder-length.
3. never dyes his hair.
4. either shaves every day or keeps his facial hair short and neat.
5. takes care of his skin by using a good cleanser and face lotion.
6. wears sunscreen to protect his skin and to avoid looking older.
7. knows that makeup is usually for women, not men—but he may use it to hide acne.
8. is pampered at the spa once in a while but not too often.

Reader Comments

 charles23   20 minutes ago
Most of these tips are smart. I started using a cleanser, and my skin is a lot clearer. And sunscreen is important. But I'm not sure about the hair advice. What's wrong with long or dyed hair?

 LADavid   33 minutes ago
This writer thinks too much about his looks. No one cares if a man clips his nails or if he shaves every day. And skin products and spas are for women, aren't they?

1. What should a man never do with his nails, according to the blog writer?
2. How can a man stay young-looking?
3. According to the blog's writer, when is it okay for a man to wear makeup?
4. Which commenter agrees more with the writer?

Now Write

Write a response to this blog writer.

_____
_____
_____
_____

A Vocabulary

Complete the crossword.

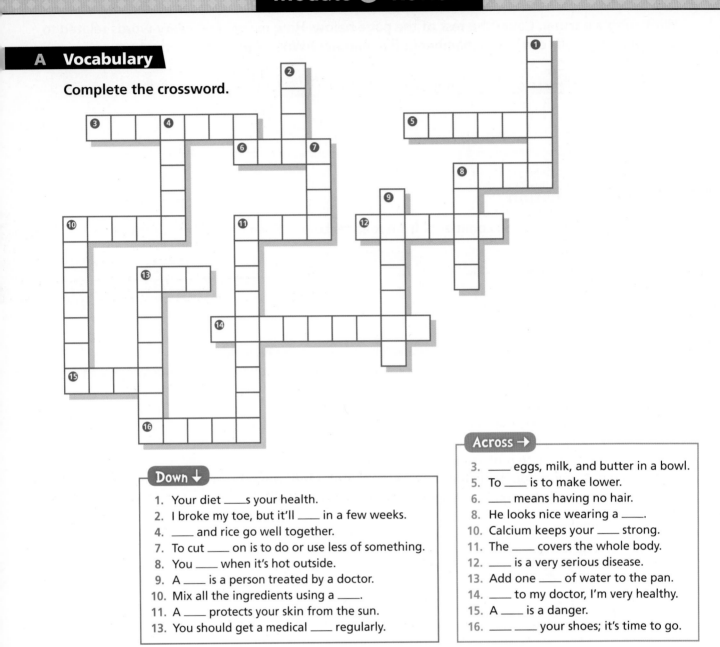

Down ↓

1. Your diet ____s your health.
2. I broke my toe, but it'll ____ in a few weeks.
4. ____ and rice go well together.
7. To cut ____ on is to do or use less of something.
8. You ____ when it's hot outside.
9. A ____ is a person treated by a doctor.
10. Mix all the ingredients using a ____.
11. A ____ protects your skin from the sun.
13. You should get a medical ____ regularly.

Across →

3. ____ eggs, milk, and butter in a bowl.
5. To ____ is to make lower.
6. ____ means having no hair.
8. He looks nice wearing a ____.
10. Calcium keeps your ____ strong.
11. The ____ covers the whole body.
12. ____ is a very serious disease.
13. Add one ____ of water to the pan.
14. ____ to my doctor, I'm very healthy.
15. A ____ is a danger.
16. ____ ____ your shoes; it's time to go.

B Grammar

Look back at the module. Fill in the blanks.

1. Your brother lives here, _____ _____?

2. The dentist said _____ floss every day.

3. _____n't Mr. Yoo over there?

4. I can't see _____ his hair is red or not.

5. _____ you eat right, _____ feel good.

6. My doctor always says _____ people need to exercise for 60 minutes every day.

7. For a mud bath, you are _____ in mud.

8. She isn't at the spa, _____ _____?

9. I took this photo. → It was _____ by me.

10. If people _____ eat enough, they lose weight.

11. How was your trip? Tell me _____ it!

12. His mood _____ improve if he exercises.

13. "When can you come?" → She asked when _____ _____ come.

14. Tea _____ served at the salon every day.

15. "Open your books," he said to us. → He told _____ _____ open our books.

16. "What time is it?" → I don't know what time _____ _____.

C Discuss

Talk about these questions in small groups: When was the last time you cooked? What did you make? What were the ingredients? How did it taste?

D A Healthy Plan of Action

Jeff wants to feel and look better. With a partner, create a plan of action to help Jeff. **Person A should create an exercise routine for Jeff, as well as a personal hygiene and grooming plan. Write it in the space provided.** (Person B should listen to Person A's routine and plan for Jeff and write it in the space.)

Person B should think of two recipes for healthy meals that Jeff can make at home. Write the recipes in the space provided. (Person A should listen to Person B's recipes and write them in the space.)

Recipe #1

Recipe #2

If you can, try the recipes at home!

Out of Town

Module 4 Goals

Understand instructions expressed in simple language (for example, how to use public telephones or ticket machines, safety information, or directions)

Understand the main points of discussion on familiar topics in everyday situations

Give a short, prepared presentation on a country, a sports team, a band, etc., and answer questions clearly

Write a short, formal email asking for or giving simple information

Write simple texts about experiences or events (for example, describing your feelings and reactions about a trip)

Understand information in announcements

Make routine phone calls (for example, making or canceling an order, booking, or appointment)

Preview

Look at pages 92 to 117. What pages are these things on?

a red car   _____

a menu   _____

a train car   _____

a video game store   _____

Discuss

Talk about the questions with a partner.

1. Where do you think the person in the picture has traveled to?

2. What kinds of things do you think visitors do there?

3. Do you enjoy traveling? Why or why not?

4. Where did you go on your last trip?

5. How did you prepare for your trip?

Write

Choose one of the questions from above. Write a couple of sentences to answer it.

_____

_____

_____

Unit 7

Unit 8

Scan the QR code to watch a preview video.

| Lesson 1 | I'll take the non-stop flight. |

A Model Conversation

Read the conversation. Then listen. 🔊 Track 47

Helen: Hey, Paulo, I'm booking the flights for us and Dana. Do you want to check the information first?

Paulo: Okay. So, you're booking three round-trip tickets to New York, right?

Helen: Right.

Paulo: There are a lot of airports in New York City. Which one is our destination?

Helen: LaGuardia.

Paulo: And we're departing on the 28th? Hmm. I don't know...

Helen: Is that a problem?

Paulo: It's a Friday. Airfares are more expensive on weekends. If we fly on Wednesday or Thursday, it would be cheaper.

Helen: I know, but the flights available on those days are fully booked.

Paulo: Ah, okay. I see there's a three-hour layover. How much are the direct flights?

Helen: They start at $70 more.

Paulo: That's not too bad. If it means we don't have to wait three hours for a connection, I think it's worth it.

Helen: Okay. I'll book this one. Three economy-class tickets. Do you want a window or aisle seat?

Paulo: I'll take the aisle.

> **Brief note**
> "Economy class" is sometimes called coach.

B Vocabulary

Match each word or phrase with the correct definition.

1. round-trip •
2. direct/non-stop •
3. layover •
4. airfare •
5. connection •
6. economy class •
7. depart •
8. destination •

• a. a stop during a long trip
• b. the cheapest kind of seat on a plane
• c. without stopping
• d. to leave to go on a trip or journey
• e. traveling to a place and back
• f. the place you are going to
• g. when you get off one flight and onto another
• h. the cost of an airplane ticket

C Vocabulary Comprehension

Fill in the blanks with the correct words from above.

Hi, Dana.

Paulo and I booked three ❶ _____ tickets for New York, leaving on the 28th! I'm emailing your e-ticket to you. Good news—it's a ❷ _____ flight. There was a cheaper flight with a ❸ _____, but it's better to fly non-stop. And the ❹ _____ for that other flight was only $70 less.

You'll also be happy to know that Paulo is taking the ❺ _____ _____, so you can have the window seat. Looking forward to the trip!

Best,
Helen

D Grammar

Second conditional

second conditional		
Second conditional sentences are *if* sentences about a hypothetical (unreal) situation. The first conditional (see Unit 5, lesson 5) is about something that is probable in the future. The second conditional is about something that is not true in the present or something that is less probable in the future.		
Second conditional sentences have the form *If* + subject + simple past verb phrase, (*then*) subject + *would* + verb phrase.		
if clause: condition	*would* clause: result ←	(+ extra information)
If I **were** rich, If she **took** a relaxing trip, If we **didn't have** exams next week,	I **would** / I**'d travel** around the world. then her health **would get** better. we **would** / we**'d stay** in Mexico longer.	(I'm not rich.) (She has no plans to take a trip.) (We do have exams next week.)
The *would* clause can come first. No comma is needed in this case.		
I**'d travel** around the world if I **were** rich. My friends **would be** upset if we **missed** our connection.		

Brief note

In the second conditional, the use of *were* with singular subjects is considered correct: *If I/he/she **were** rich, ...* But it's okay to use *was* informally: *If I/he/she **was** rich, ...*

Brief note

In the result clause, you can use *could* instead of *would* to talk about possibilities: *If we **didn't have** exams next week, we **could stay** in Mexico longer.*

E Grammar Practice

Circle the correct answers.

1. (Whether / If) they took the train, the trip would take much longer.

2. If I could travel anywhere, I would probably (go / going) to France.

3. If Robert (didn't / doesn't) have to work today, he could drive you to the airport.

4. If I (were / would be) in a window seat, I'd be able to sleep.

5. I would definitely fly Korean Air if I (had / have) a choice.

6. Jenny wouldn't get angry if her sister's flight (arriving / arrived) late.

7. Our flight to London (was / would be) cheaper if we traveled on a weekday.

F Use the Language

Booking a flight

You and your partner are planning to take a trip. First, agree on a destination. Then write a conversation in which you are calling to book a flight. Perform your conversation for the class.

_____

_____

_____

_____

_____

_____

_____

_____

93

A   Model Monologue

Read the monologue. Then listen. Discuss the questions below with a partner. Track 48

Brad: My brother Jim and I are planning to take a vacation together and drive across the country. We'll stop overnight in a few cities on the way, but we cannot agree on where to stay. I want to save money and stay in inexpensive motel rooms. A comfortable double room with air-conditioning is good enough for me. We could check out early in the morning, buy food at the supermarket, and then continue driving. We used to do this on family trips when we were children.

Jim prefers to book nice hotel suites with lots of amenities. He has stayed in many nice hotels because of his old job. When he traveled for his job, he would swim in the pool, exercise in the gym, order room service, and eat in the hotel restaurant. He says he wouldn't mind the expense, but I think it's silly to waste so much money on a one-night stay.

Discuss

1. What are the benefits of staying in a hotel? A motel?
2. Which one would you prefer, a hotel or a motel?

B   Vocabulary

Listen to Jim making a reservation. Fill in the blanks with the correct words and phrases from the box. (Three will not be used.) Track 49

vacation	overnight	comfortable	suite	double room
air-conditioning	amenities	inexpensive	room service	check out

1. Jim chooses to book a(n) _____ _____ rather than a(n) _____.

2. They will stay _____ and _____ _____ on June 15th.

3. The room comes with many _____, including air-conditioning and _____ _____.

4. Internet service at the hotel is not free, but it's pretty _____.

C   In Your World

Tell your partner about a hotel or motel you have stayed in. Say whether you would recommend it or not, and explain why. Take notes on your partner's experience and describe it to the class.

_____
_____
_____
_____
_____

D | Grammar

would and *used to*

Brief note

Used to can also be used to talk about past states, with stative verbs such as *be, have, like, own*, etc. *Would* cannot be used with stative verbs.
(✓) My hair **used to be** long. / She **used to have** a dog.
(X) My hair **would be** long. / She **would have** a dog.

would and *used to*		
Both *would* + verb and *used to* + verb can be used to talk about habits or repeated actions in the past. They describe things that often or regularly happened in the past, but no longer happen.		
statement	My grandmother **would bake** cookies for us. We **would travel** to Guadalajara in the spring.	Sean **used to stay** at a hotel in London. The Faber family **used to fly** to Italy once a year.
negative	We **wouldn't** usually **take** expensive trips. I **wouldn't shop** much when I was on vacation.	That hotel **didn't use to charge** a parking fee! We **didn't use to travel** in the summer when we were kids.
question	**Would** they **drive** all night or stop at a motel? Where **would** you **go** on those long bike rides?	**Did** she **use to book** a room in advance or just show up? What **did** you **use to do** on weekends?

Brief note

In negatives and questions using the auxiliary verb *do*, the correct form is *use to*.

E | Grammar Practice

Read the article. Fill in the blanks with *would* or *used to* and the correct form of the given verb. (For some blanks, more than one answer is possible.)

The History of Motels

Highways ❶ _____ (were) rare in North America until the 1920s. Before then, people ❷ _____ (didn't take) long car trips often. When they did go on long trips, they ❸ _____ (slept) in their cars.

In the 1920s, highways became more common. Smart businesspeople ❹ _____ (built) small, simple hotels near highways for travelers. These hotels were called motor hotels, or motels. The owners ❺ _____ (put) free parking spaces right next to the rooms.

Motels ❻ _____ (were) even more popular than they are today. They were most popular in the 1950s and 1960s. Most motels ❼ _____ (were owned) by one person or family. Now most of them are owned by big companies.

F | Listen to Speak

Listen to the conversation between a motel clerk and a customer. Then read the statements and circle true or false. 🎧 **Track 50**

1.	The man's family used to visit the Green Lake Motel.	true	false
2.	The man would go swimming in the motel pool in the past.	true	false
3.	The motel didn't use to have a restaurant.	true	false
4.	As a kid, the man would enjoy the view of the lake.	true	false
5.	The motel's amenities now include breakfast and boat rental.	true	false
6.	The man decides to book one double room for one night.	true	false

Now role-play a telephone conversation with a partner. You are making a motel or hotel booking, and you have questions about the types of rooms available, amenities, and costs. Take turns being the customer and the motel or hotel clerk.

A | Authentic Text: Car rental and car sharing

Read the article. Then listen. Discuss the question below with a partner. Track 51

Car Rental and Car Sharing: **Pros and Cons**

You're on a trip to a new city without a car. You'd rather not use public transportation because you're used to driving yourself. So you can either rent a car or use a car **sharing** service. Which is the best way to **get around**?

Car Rental: You can easily find big car rental companies in every city and at every airport. They allow you to choose and reserve cars **in advance**, and the cars are cleaned and checked after each rental. These are the pros.

The cons: You must rent by the day. It's expensive, and it might not **be worth it** for a short trip. **Plus**, you have to wait in line at the rental office to get the **keys**.

Car Sharing: This is a new kind of service, so not everyone has gotten used to it yet. People use a smartphone app to **lend** their cars to other drivers. The borrower pays by the hour. The app tells the borrower where the car is parked and allows him or her to **unlock** it. (The owner leaves the keys inside.) It's **convenient** because you can borrow a car for a short time, and you don't have to wait in line.

The cons: You can't always reserve a car in advance, and it's hard to get one during busy times of day. Also, the car might not be in great shape.

Brief note

Use "by the (time)" to say what unit of time is used when renting something or buying a service.
Personal trainers charge by the hour.

You can rent a room by the night or by the week.

Discuss: Can you think of any more pros and cons for car rental and car sharing?

B | Vocabulary

Write the bold words and phrases from part A next to the correct definitions.

1. _____ also; in addition
2. _____ using something together with other people
3. _____ able to be done without much trouble
4. _____ good points and bad points; advantages and disadvantages
5. _____ to give (something to someone) to use for a certain amount of time
6. _____ before the actual time; early
7. _____ to go from place to place
8. _____ to open the lock on something (A lock keeps something, such as a door, closed.)
9. _____ small pieces of metal that are used to open or gain entry to something
10. _____ to be good or useful enough for the price; to be a good deal

C | In Your World

In a small group, choose a nearby city you want to visit together for the weekend. Plan your trip by agreeing on answers to the following questions. Explain your answers and reasons to the class.

TO-DO LIST

1. Will you take a group member's car, rent a car, or use a car-sharing service?
2. Who will drive?
3. Where will you stay?

D   Grammar

be used to and get used to

used to + verb	be used to + noun/gerund	get used to + noun/gerund
used to describe a past habit or repeated action	to be familiar and comfortable with something	to become familiar and comfortable with something
Marion **used to be** an accountant. We **used to have** a hatchback. They **didn't use to take** vacations. **Did** he **use to work** at Quick Cars?	I'm **used to** riding a crowded bus. Canadians **are used to** cold winters. My sister **isn't used to** driving. **Is** Sammy **used to** sleeping on the floor?	John's **getting used to** sharing his car. You'll **get used to** the new apartment. I never **got used to** living in Alaska. What was the hardest part to **get used to**?

E   Grammar Practice

Circle the correct answers.

1. Zoe (is used to / used to) borrow her older sister's car before she got her own.
2. You'll (used to / get used to) sharing your office with a coworker.
3. After a month, Antonio (is used to / used to) his new school.
4. It's a new car. I haven't (gotten used to / been used to) driving it yet.

Put the words in order to make sentences.

5. used / by / around / he's / getting / bus / to

   _____ .

6. getting / to / car / we / long / trips / very / used / are

   _____ .

7. Shelly / used / in / staying / won't / to / motels / get / inexpensive

   _____ .

F   Read to Write

Read the following article giving advice to international student visitors. Fill in the blanks with the correct words and phrases from the box. Then listen and check your answers. 🔊 Track 52

in advance	get used to	plus	be used to	get around	worth it

> **Congratulations on choosing Trent College for your study abroad! Here are some quick tips before you get on the plane.**
>
> - Rent an apartment ❶ _____ _____ . Don't wait until you come here. It could take a while. ❷ _____ , hotels aren't cheap. Go to the housing office website for help.
> - Think about how you'll ❸ _____ _____ the city. You might ❹ _____ _____ _____ using public transportation at home, but the buses aren't very convenient in Trent. It might be ❺ _____ _____ to buy an inexpensive car or to rent one by the month. If you don't drive, you can also try the college's ride-sharing service.
> - Get ready for winter! Many international students say that the cold weather is the hardest thing to ❻ _____ _____ _____ . Bring lots of warm clothes or enough money to buy them here.

On a separate sheet of paper, write a few tips for young people visiting your town from abroad. What do they need to know and do in advance? What will they need to get used to? Share your tips with the class.

A   Model Conversation

Read the conversation. Then listen. Track 53

Pierre: Where do you want to go to celebrate your birthday on Friday?

Teresa: Well, I heard there's a terrific new Thai restaurant on Packard Avenue. It's called Sunset Thai.

Pierre: Oh, yeah. It gets really good reviews online. Amazing food. Great service. Beautiful décor.

Teresa: I know. Everyone is raving about it!

Pierre: I heard that the chef at Sunset Thai used to work at The Spice Restaurant.

Teresa: Then the food will be delicious for sure! And I heard the patio is gorgeous.

Pierre: Let's make a reservation right now, in case it gets fully booked.

Teresa: Okay. Table for two for Friday at 7 p.m. On the patio, of course!

B   Vocabulary

Match each word with the correct definition.

1. celebrate
2. terrific
3. server
4. décor
5. rave
6. chef
7. patio
8. gorgeous

a. to talk about how wonderful something is
b. a waiter or waitress
c. to do something special for an important event
d. an outdoor area attached to a home or restaurant
e. very good; excellent
f. extremely beautiful
g. how the inside of a building looks: the furniture, pictures on the walls, etc.
h. a professional cook

C   Vocabulary Comprehension

Circle the correct answers.

1. It's too cold to sit out on the (décor / patio) tonight.
2. The menu is completely different. Maybe they hired a new (server / chef).
3. The service at that new Italian place is (gorgeous / terrific).
4. I love the (décor / server) here. It feels like we're actually in a restaurant in Paris.
5. We're here to (rave / celebrate) my sister's graduation.
6. We're ready to order. Where is our (server / chef)?
7. My friend Celine recommends getting the seafood pasta. She just (raves / celebrates) about it.

D Grammar

Reported speech with *I heard*

You may use the word *that* after *I heard*. This is optional.

reported speech with *I heard*	
Reported speech using *I heard* does not focus on where the information came from, so it is less reliable or trustworthy.	Other reported speech focuses more on where the information came from and is generally more reliable and trustworthy.
I heard that the new Italian restaurant is awful! We **heard** there's a big sale at the bookstore today. Jason said he **heard** there's a party at Tatiana's tonight. **Did** you **hear that** Maryanne got a new boyfriend?	I read a really bad online review of the new Italian restaurant. We got an ad in the mail about a big sale at the bookstore. Tatiana invited Jason to a party at her apartment tonight. Did Maryanne tell you that she got a new boyfriend?

E Grammar Practice

Put a check mark next to the correct description of each statement.

1. Fred told me that he is leaving the company. ☐ more reliable ☐ less reliable

2. I heard the pizza place on the corner is closing. ☐ more reliable ☐ less reliable

3. We heard that going downtown is dangerous. ☐ more reliable ☐ less reliable

4. *The York Daily* said the celebration is canceled. ☐ more reliable ☐ less reliable

5. My professor told me that there's a meeting on Monday. ☐ more reliable ☐ less reliable

6. I heard Martin and Hawa are getting a divorce. ☐ more reliable ☐ less reliable

F Use the Language

What have you heard about this restaurant?

Think of three restaurants in your town that are known by name to most of your classmates. (You may or may not have eaten at these places yourself.) List them on the left in the table below.

Restaurant	Person #1	Person #2	Person #3
1.			
2.			
3.			

Now ask three classmates about the restaurants. They may give their own opinions or report what they've heard. Make notes of their answers. Report to the class what you found out. Would you recommend any of the restaurants?

A Model Conversation

Read the conversation. Then listen. Complete the exercise below. ⊙ Track 54

Chad: I heard you had your first date with Rob on Saturday. How did it go?

Angela: Not bad, but it didn't go totally smoothly.

Chad: Uh-oh. What happened? You went to the movies, right?

Angela: Yeah. I booked the tickets online for the 7 o'clock showing at the Sunrise Theater downtown. We agreed to meet there early so we could have coffee first. But by ten to seven, Rob hadn't shown up. And my cell phone had died.

Chad: Oh, no. What did you do?

Angela: The guy at the box office let me charge my phone, and I called Rob. He'd gone to the wrong theater.

Chad: Ah, he went to the Sunrise Theater at the mall, didn't he?

Angela: Exactly. So I told him to hurry and meet me downtown. By the time he arrived, the movie had started. We missed the first ten minutes.

Chad: I bet Rob was upset.

Angela: He was pretty embarrassed. But the movie was funny, so he'd cheered up by the end.

Number these events from 1 to 5 in the order that they happened.

____ Angela called Rob.   ____ Rob arrived at the right theater.

____ The movie started.   ____ It was 6:50.   ____ Angela charged her phone.

B Vocabulary

Write the words and phrases from the box next to the correct definitions.

| smoothly | showing | box office | mall | hurry | exactly | embarrassed | cheer up |

1. _____ to move, go, or act quickly
2. _____ feeling confused and silly in front of other people
3. _____ without problems or difficulties
4. _____ to start to feel happier; to be in a better mood
5. _____ a large building with many kinds of stores inside
6. _____ the act of making a movie, TV show, etc., available for people to see
7. _____ a word used to say that someone is correct or that you agree completely
8. _____ the place at a theater where people buy tickets

C About You

Think about the last movie you saw at a movie theater. Discuss the following questions with a partner.

- What kind of movie was it, and what was the title?
- Where did you see it?
- Who did you see it with?
- How did you purchase the tickets to this show?
- Would you recommend this movie to others? Why or why not?

D Grammar

Past perfect tense

Brief note

The past perfect clause can also come first.
No comma is needed in that case.
*The movie **had started** by the time he arrived.*

past perfect	
The past perfect tense is used to talk about an action that was finished before something else happened in the past. The past perfect has the form *had* + past participle. *Had* is often shortened to *-'d* after pronouns.	
the action happened before a specific past time (often with *at/by* + time)	He didn't show up. It was five to seven (then). → At five to seven, he **hadn't shown up**.
	It stopped raining before 4:30. → By 4:30, it **had stopped** raining.
the action happened before a specific event (often with a simple past clause using *by the time* or *when*)	They went to bed. Then I got home. → When I got home, they **had** / they**'d** (already) **gone** to bed.
	The movie started. Then he arrived. → By the time he arrived, the movie **had** (already) started.

E Grammar Practice

Circle the correct answers.

1. Josephine still (didn't call / hadn't called) by 11 o'clock last night.
2. A: Why didn't Max join you for the movie last night?
   B: He'd already (saw / seen) it.
3. By the time we left the theater, the sun (came / had come) out.
4. When I (met / had met) my friend at the box office, (she / she'd) already bought the tickets.

Combine the sentences using the words in parentheses and the past perfect.

5. He spent all his money. Then we left the mall. (by the time)

   _____

6. We didn't eat all our popcorn. Then the movie ended. (when)

   _____

7. You started eating. Then I walked into the restaurant. (when, already)

   _____

F Listen to Write

You are at a movie theater box office waiting for a friend. You have already bought tickets. Then you hear an announcement about the film you were going to see. Listen to the announcement and then write a text to your friend explaining the problem. Track 55

A. Confirming Your Flight Details

Below are flight details from your travel agent. Read the statements and put a check mark next to true or false.

Lucky Travels Inc.　　　　　　**Flight Confirmation**

Name: Margaret Emily Rose　　　**Date of Birth**: December 2, 1979　　　**Nationality**: Canadian
Departure: September 12, 9:15 a.m., from Toronto Pearson International Airport (YYZ)
　　　　　　Flight AC2045 (Non-stop)
Arrival: September 12, 11:30 a.m., Hartsfield-Jackson Atlanta International Airport (ATL)

Please arrive at Terminal 1 at least 2.5 hours before your flight. Reserve seats and check in with Air Canada online at www.pia.ca. There is a limit of one carry-on and one checked bag per passenger.

---

1. This is a round-trip ticket confirmation.　　　☐ true ☐ false
2. The destination is Atlanta, Georgia.　　　☐ true ☐ false
3. There is a layover during the trip.　　　☐ true ☐ false
4. The flight is two hours and fifteen minutes long.　☐ true ☐ false
5. The airfare is stated.　　　☐ true ☐ false

B. Canceling Your Flight

You have decided to cancel your flight and change it to another day. With a partner, role-play a conversation between Margaret and her travel agent. Then write the confirmation details of your new flight below.

Lucky Travels Inc.
Flight Confirmation

Name: Margaret Emily Rose
Date of Birth: December 2, 1979
Nationality: Canadian
Departure: _____
Arrival: _____

Please arrive at Terminal 1 at least 2.5 hours before your flight. Reserve seats and check in with Air Canada online at www.pia.ca. There is a limit of one carry-on and one checked bag per passenger.

C. Reminder

Some Module 4 Goals in Unit 7

Put a check mark (✓) next to the things you can do.

_____ Understand the main points of discussion on familiar topics in everyday situations

_____ Give a short, prepared presentation on a country, a sports team, a band, etc., and answer questions clearly

_____ Understand information in announcements

_____ Make routine phone calls (for example, making or canceling an order, booking, or appointment)

A Read to Speak

You and your friends are planning a one-week trip to London, England, on the first of next month. Look up some information online about flights, accommodations, and car rental/sharing services. Make brief notes about the best options you find.

Flight	Accommodations	Car
Flight #: Departure: Direct or layover? Arrival: Airfare:	Hotel or motel? Name: Area in London: Amenities: Type of room: Cost per night:	Company Name (if renting): Cost per day: App name (if car sharing): Cost per hour:

B Write to Speak

Now prepare to explain your choices to your friends. Write why you think that if your group followed your plan, things would work out very well during your trip.

1. If we took this flight…

   _____

   _____

2. If we stayed in these accommodations…

   _____

   _____

3. If we rented a car from this agency… / If we used this car-sharing service…

   _____

   _____

C Now Speak

In your group, let each person explain their choices and reasons. After each presentation, group members may ask questions and state their opinions about why they agree or disagree. By the end of the discussion, your group should make a final decision about the details of this trip.

Flight	Accommodations	Car

Lesson 1	The Best Shopping in Town

Brief note

A *vendor* is a seller. "Street vendors" are people who sell things outside on the street rather than inside a building.

A Authentic Text: Shopping guide

Read part of a tourist information brochure about shopping in San Francisco. Which of these places would you most like to visit?

SAN FRANCISCO SHOPPING GUIDE

1 North Beach
Don't miss out on San Francisco's well-known Italian district, with an *Italiano* style that you can see and taste! Visit fashionable shops offering clothing, accessories, and home décor. And when you're done, enjoy authentic Italian food at one of the many fine restaurants in the area.

2 Union Square
This downtown district is the number-one destination for both local shoppers and tourists. Shop around for men's and women's clothing, accessories, beauty products, electronics, and more. If you ever get tired of shopping, you can check out some of Union Square's many theaters, art galleries, salons, or hotels.

3 Chinatown
Not far from North Beach, there's a little piece of China. You will feel like you're in Shanghai as you explore shops with a huge selection of imports, from furniture to tea. From the area's many street vendors, you can also pick up fun souvenirs and some delicious but inexpensive Chinese cuisine.

B Vocabulary

Match the words and phrases with the correct definitions.

1. accessory •   • a. brought from one country to another for sale
2. electronics •   • b. a certain area or neighborhood in a city
3. get tired of •   • c. something you buy to remember a place you visited
4. district •   • d. a number of different choices
5. genuine •   • e. products that use electricity, such as TVs, computers, cell phones, etc.
6. fashionable •   • f. cooking; food
7. selection •   • g. something you wear besides clothes, such as a hat, a scarf, a bag, etc.
8. imported •   • h. showing taste and style (in clothes, hair, etc.) that is popular now
9. souvenir •   • i. real; true; not copied or false
10. cuisine •   • j. to become bored or impatient with (something)

C About You

Think of the last time you visited a popular shopping area. What was it like? Did you buy anything? Tell a partner, and answer his or her questions. Listen to your partner's experience and ask questions.

Grammar

Phrasal verbs

phrasal verbs		
Phrasal verbs are made up of a verb plus one or more particles (words that look like prepositions or adverbs): for example, *hang out*. Phrasal verbs are most common in informal speech and writing. There are two main types: inseparable and separable.		
	examples	**sentences**
inseparable There is no object between the verb and the particle(s).	*hang out, drop by, get around, shop around (for), miss out (on), log in/out, sign in/out*	Let's **hang out** at the mall. Don't **miss out on** this amazing sale. I want to **shop around for** phones before I buy one. **Drop by** our store to get a great deal on shoes.
separable The object may come between the verb and the particle.	*turn on/off, pick up, think over, throw away, look up, find out, check out, put on, take off, drop off*	Did you **pick up** some school supplies? Did you **pick** them **up**? We should **check** Chinatown **out** before we go. We should **check** it **out** before we go.

Grammar Practice

Fill in the blanks with one of the phrasal verbs from above. Use a dictionary to help you if necessary.

1. My mom used to _____ me _____ at school every morning.

2. I'm going to _____ my shoes _____ because they're uncomfortable.

3. It's getting cold. You should _____ _____ your sweater.

4. If you don't come to the party, you'll _____ _____ _____ a fun evening.

Underline the error and write the correct phrase. If the sentence is correct, write *correct*.

5. I didn't know the meaning of this word, so I looked up it. _____

6. He uses the subway to get town around. _____

7. No one is watching TV, so please turn off it. _____

8. My parents are out of town. Want to hang it out? _____

Use the Language

Partners in business

Working in pairs or small groups, pick a business, store, or restaurant that you are familiar with. Discuss the details of this business, including the following:

- Its name
- Its location
- The kind of food/products it sells
- Its pricing (expensive or inexpensive)
- Its selling points (how it's different and why people will like it)

Then write a radio advertisement (5–7 sentences) for the business, store, or restaurant you chose. One partner will read your advertisement to the class. Both or all partners should be ready to answer questions from your classmates!

A Model Conversation

Read the conversation. Then listen. 🔊 Track 56

Kevin: We have a few hours before our flight. Why don't we do some shopping? We haven't spent much time in Union Square yet.

Tori: Well, okay, as long as you're sure we have enough time. We still need to pick up our luggage at the hotel and drop the rental car off.

Kevin: Don't worry; there's plenty of time. I need to get some souvenirs for my family. Otherwise, I know they'll be upset with me. Should we drive?

Tori: No, it's almost **rush hour**. Plus, I heard it's really hard to find parking. What about a streetcar?

Kevin: Too slow. Let's take the BART. Here, I found the map online. We can get on at the station across the street and take the yellow **line** to Powell Street. Then, we can walk to Union Square. We don't even need to **transfer**.

Tori: Great. How much is the **fare**?

Kevin: That **depends on** the distance. The ticket machine will **calculate** that for us.

Tori: All right, let's get going. Unless we leave right now, we'll be **stuck** in a crowded train with all the **commuters**!

> **Brief note**
> The Bay Area Rapid Transit or "BART" is a light rail public transportation that operates in San Francisco.

B Vocabulary

Read the conversation again. With a partner, match the bold words in the conversation to the correct definitions.

1. _____ in a difficult situation that is hard to get out of
2. _____ to find a number using math
3. _____ is determined by (something)
4. _____ people traveling to or from work
5. _____ to change from one bus, train, etc., to another
6. _____ the time of day when many people are going to or from work
7. _____ a part of a subway or bus system; a certain train or bus route
8. _____ the cost of taking a bus, train, etc.

C Vocabulary Comprehension

Look at the map and fill in the blanks in the conversation below. Then listen and check your answers. 🔊 Track 57

Man: Excuse me. Can I take the subway from the Expo Center to the airport?

Woman: Sure. The ❶ _____ line goes to Union Station. There, you can ❷ _____ to the ❸ _____ line. Then go ❹ _____ stops to Gateway Station. Transfer to the ❺ _____ line and go one more stop.

Man: Thanks. What's the ❻ _____?

Woman: That ❼ _____ _____ whether you want a one-way or round-trip ticket.

(Map showing stations: Expo Center, Airport, Rose Quarter, Union Station, Gateway, Pioneer Square, Gresham, PSU, Overton, Clackamas Town Center, Milwaukie, with WILLAMETTE RIVER)

With a partner, practice the conversation. Then take turns choosing two stations on the map and asking your partner for directions from one station to the other.

D Grammar

Ways to express conditions

Brief note

As with other subordinating conjunctions, the two clauses can come in either order.
***As long as** you're sure we have enough time, we can go shopping.*
*We'll be stuck with all the commuters **unless** we leave right now!*

ways to express conditions		
Besides the word *if*, there are several ways to talk about conditions in English.		
expression	meaning	example
as long as / so long as (conjunctions)	(only) if	We can go shopping **as long as** you're sure we have enough time. (= ... if you're sure we have enough time.)
unless (conjunction)	if not ... then	**Unless** we leave right now, we'll be stuck with all the commuters! (= If we don't leave right now, ...)
otherwise (sentence adverb)	if not	I have to get souvenirs for my family. **Otherwise**, they'll be upset. (= ... If not, they'll be upset.)

E Grammar Practice

Fill in the blanks with the correct expressions from above.

1. _____ we remember to take an umbrella, we should be okay!

2. You should try to leave by four. _____, you'll get stuck in rush-hour traffic.

3. _____ the subway is on time, we'll make it to the movie.

4. _____ you study harder, you won't pass your final exam.

5. You can borrow my car _____ you return it by midnight.

6. We'll have to cancel the trip _____ the weather improves.

7. She has to take a taxi, not the bus. _____, she'll be late.

8. _____ it all goes smoothly, the show will be a success.

Rewrite the sentences using the given expression.

9. The bus is free if you have a student ID. (as long as)

_____

10. If I don't find my keys, I won't be able to give you a ride. (unless)

_____

F Use the Language

Subway systems

1. Go online and find a map of a subway, tube, or metro system in another city or country. Describe where it is and give your opinion of it. Does it seem convenient? Does it seem difficult to use? How does it compare to the subway system in your city or country?

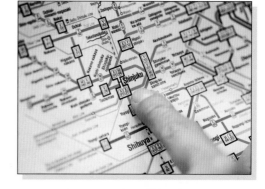

2. With a partner, design a subway map for your city or make suggestions to improve your city's subway system. If you could design a whole new subway system to make travel more convenient in your city, what would you do? What would it look like? Draw it and present it to another pair of students. Explain the reasons for your decisions.

A Model Conversation

Read the conversation. Then listen. ◉ Track 58

Anna: So, are you done with your shopping?

Eric: Yep, I am, and that's good because I've run out of money. Did you get to see the whole mall? This place is enormous. I'd love it if we had a mall like this back home.

Anna: No, I couldn't. And I knew you would love this place, especially with all the cool electronics stores. That reminds me—I have one more purchase to make. I've been planning to get a fitness tracker for my dad.

Eric: Really? Is he into fitness?

Anna: Well, a month ago his doctor told him to exercise more and lose weight. So he's been taking long walks every day. But he doesn't really enjoy it.

Eric: So you think that if he could see how many steps he's taking, it might encourage him to keep going?

Anna: Exactly. And I think he'd appreciate it. He's like you—he loves all electronic devices. They're like toys for him.

Eric: Okay, then let's hurry and pick one out. I've been keeping an eye on the time, and the mall closes in twenty minutes.

B Vocabulary

Listen to each word or phrase. Then write each word next to the correct definition. ◉ Track 59

run out of	enormous	purchase	remind	encourage	appreciate	device	keep an eye on

1. _____ something bought

2. _____ a machine or piece of equipment designed for a specific purpose

3. _____ to use up something so that you no longer have any

4. _____ to check regularly; to watch carefully

5. _____ to cause someone to remember something

6. _____ to be thankful for something and understand its importance or value

7. _____ extremely big

8. _____ to make someone more likely to do something

C In Your World

Ask a partner the following questions. Discuss the answers and share the most interesting things with another pair of students.

- Do you enjoy shopping for electronic devices? When did you last purchase one? What was it?

- Do you shop at a mall? What is your favorite store there?

- Do you prefer shopping in stores or online? Why?

- If you were very rich, how would your shopping habits change?

Grammar

Present perfect continuous tense

present perfect continuous	
The present perfect continuous is similar to the present perfect. Both tenses are used to talk about actions that began at some time in the past and are connected to the present. With the present perfect continuous, the focus is on the process. The action is or was ongoing, and either is not finished or has recently finished. This tense has the form *have/has* + *been* + present participle.	
the action has been ongoing and is not finished	I've **been planning** to get my dad a fitness tracker. (I still am.) It's **been raining** since early this morning. (It still is.) They **haven't been keeping** an eye on the time. (They still aren't.) How long **have** you **been living** here? (You still are.)
the action has been ongoing and has recently finished	It's nice to finally sit down. I've **been shopping** all day. Her eyes are red. I think she's **been crying**. You're covered with sweat. **Have** you **been exercising**? The kitchen smells wonderful. Someone's **been cooking**.

Grammar Practice

Circle the correct answers. Then read your answers out loud to your partner.

1. (We've / We're) been having a great time on this vacation!

2. He (haven't / hasn't) been learning English for very long.

3. I've been (waiting / wait) for you for the last five hours!

4. Have (been you and Doug / you and Doug been) dating this past year?

Fill in the blanks with the correct forms of the given verbs in the present perfect continuous.

5. I'm healthier because I _____ (use) a fitness tracker for a while.

6. He _____ (remind) me about his birthday for two weeks!

7. How long _____ you _____ (work) at the mall?

Use the Language

Talking about your devices

Interview a partner about technology that they use. It could be a phone, a computer, a tablet, an MP3 player, etc. Ask them 5–10 questions about the device, including where they purchased it, how long they have been using it, and whether they'd recommend that you buy one. When you think you have enough information, write about what your partner said. Do not use the name of the device. Choose another partner, and read your description out loud. Your new partner must try and guess what the device is.

Lesson 4 — A New Game

A Model Conversation

Read the conversation. Then listen. 🔴 Track 60

Brent: Hi. I'm looking for a game, but I don't know the title. I also wanted to pre-order a game and trade in a few, too.

Clerk: No problem. Let's start with the game you're looking for.

Brent: It's a new space shooting game. My brother made me play it with him during the holiday. Then he got me to promise to buy it. Sorry, I'm not much of a gamer.

Clerk: No. It's okay. One second. Here are all the newest shooting games. I think this is the one you're talking about. You can switch from first-person point of view to third-person point of view. You can also customize your character and weapons to your level.

Brent: Yeah, that's the one.

Clerk: What else can I help you with?

Brent: Right, I want to pre-order the new *Call of Duty* game.

Clerk: Okay. Just fill in this form. You also wanted to do a trade-in? Can I see the games? Hmm. Okay, well, I can give you about $30 cash for all of these or $40 of credit.

Brent: I'll take the store credit then.

B Vocabulary

Listen to each word or phrase. Then write each word next to the correct definition. 🔴 Track 61

pre-order	trade in	space	point of view	customize
character	weapon	level	cash	store credit

1. _____ to change something to fit your tastes
2. _____ to buy something by selling something else you own
3. _____ the position from which something is seen
4. _____ something (such as a gun, knife, etc.) used to fight, attack, or defend
5. _____ the area between planets, stars, and galaxies
6. _____ physical money in the form of bills and coins
7. _____ money in the form of a document that can only be used in a particular store
8. _____ a person in a movie, novel, or game
9. _____ to order an item before it is available for purchase
10. _____ a way to show one's rank, experience, or qualifications

C In Your World

Do you like to play video games? Why or why not? Who do you know that likes to play video games? Do you think playing video games is a good thing? Why or why not? Discuss with a partner and then with the class.

110

Grammar

Causative verbs

causative verbs	
The verbs *make*, *get*, and *have* can be used as causative verbs. This means you use them to talk about causing someone to do something, or causing something to happen. Causative verb phrases have the form *make/have* + object + base verb, or *get* + object + infinitive.	
make/have + object + base verb	My brother **made me play** that game. (I didn't want to play it, but my brother caused me to play it.) **I'll have the salesperson show** me something else. (I'll ask the salesperson to show me something else.)
get + object + infinitive	To **get the characters to switch** point of view, press here. (You can cause the characters to switch point of view by pressing here.)

> **Brief note**
>
> *Make* is the strongest in meaning; it usually means someone was given an order. *Have* can be used for an order or polite request. *Get* often means that a person was persuaded (talked into) doing something. It's also used for non-human objects: *I can't get my hair to stay straight*.

Grammar Practice

Underline the error and rewrite each sentence correctly.

1. He made me to wash my hands again. _____

2. I can't get my daughter go to sleep! _____

3. Can you get the car starting? _____

4. I'll has the delivery guy leave it at the door. _____

5. Can you have her to call me when she comes in? _____

6. My teacher makes us to practice new words every day. _____

7. I got my brother cleaned my room the other day. _____

8. She always makes us to feel bad about not calling her. _____

Use the Language

Writing a formal email

You recently purchased a game application for your phone. You thought all the in-game items were free, but you were charged for them unexpectedly. Write a short formal email to the company asking for an explanation and refund.

Now share your email with a partner. Write a response to your partner's email.

A Authentic Text: Safety poster

Read the safety poster.

Brief note

"Black Friday" is the biggest shopping day of the year in the US. It marks the start of holiday shopping, and it takes place after the Thanksgiving Day holiday.

This year's Black Friday Sale will start at 9 a.m. For your safety, please read the following tips:

1. Watch your surroundings. Last year's sale brought in a record number of shoppers. Be aware and cautious while shopping.
2. Do not leave your belongings unattended. Lost items can be collected at the Lost & Found. But the mall is not responsible for stolen items.
3. Keep your money, wallet, and other valuables in a safe place.
4. Know where your nearest exit is. In case of emergency, calmly proceed to exit.
5. For tourists, the duty-free exchange is located on the 2nd floor. Please bring all your receipts and items after shopping to collect your tax refund.

Thank you for shopping at Sheffield Mall. We wish you safe and happy holidays.

Attention, holiday shoppers.

B Vocabulary

Match each word with the correct definition.

1. aware
2. cautious
3. belongings
4. collect
5. receipt
6. valuable
7. emergency
8. proceed
9. exchange
10. duty-free

a. to go and get; to pick up
b. an important or expensive item that someone owns
c. a place where things are traded
d. careful; avoiding danger
e. to move in a specific direction
f. not taxed when taken out of the country
g. things a person owns
h. a paper that shows what was purchased
i. paying attention to what is happening around you
j. an unexpected problem or dangerous situation

C In Your World

With a partner, make a list of safety tips for people visiting your city. Share your list with another pair of students. Then show it to your teacher.

Grammar

Leaving out articles for brevity

leaving out articles for brevity
Sometimes, there is a need to leave out articles (*a*, *an*, *the*) to make sentences short and easy to read. On signs and posters, articles are often left out to make room for more important information. Articles are also left out in news headlines to make room for more words on the page.

Do not use the elevator. → Do not use elevator.	Proceed to the nearest exit. → Proceed to nearest exit.

A local man finds a wallet with $1,000. → Local Man Finds Wallet with $1,000 The city announces a new football stadium. → City Announces New Football Stadium

Grammar Practice

Read the safety instructions for a new laptop. Rewrite the instructions, adding articles where they have been removed.

1. Shut down laptop when not using it.

   _____

2. Turn off computer before placing into carrying bag.

   _____

3. Do not put computer directly on legs. It can burn skin. Use table or other hard surface.

   _____

4. Check fan frequently to avoid overheating.

   _____

5. Clean air vents regularly, and never put anything into air vents.

   _____

6. Do not try to clean inside of computer screen.

   _____

Quick Review

Look back at the brief notes in this module.

1. What is another word for *economy class*? _____
2. What device measures your heart rate and physical activity? _____
3. Which of the following is correct, *pick it up* or *pick up it*? _____

Use the Language

Emergency poster

1. With a partner, think of an emergency situation. Design an emergency poster for it. Be sure to include specific instructions on what to do. Make the poster as clear and concise as possible. Include images and colors that are appropriate. Go online and look at some examples to help you. Make the poster and present it to the class.

2. When you are finished, imagine that an emergency like the one described in your poster has actually happened. Write a short news article about the emergency. Include a catchy headline. Present your article to the class.

A Welcome to New York!

Read the tourist information poster. With a partner, fill in the blanks with the correct words and phrases from the box.

districts	fashionable	genuine	fare	purchase	keep an eye on
aware	cautious	get	emergency	street vendors	as long as

Welcome to New York: Tips for Tourists

People come from around the world to visit New York City. _____ _____ _____ you are _____, you will have a safe and enjoyable time here.

Stay Safe!

★ The subway is a great way to get around. But always _____ _____ _____ _____ your belongings, especially on crowded trains.

★ In subway and train stations, people may try to _____ you to give them the _____ for a ticket home. This is a common scam.

★ For your safety, be _____ of your transportation options at all times. Always find out where the nearest subway station is, so that you can catch a train quickly in an _____.

Shop Smart!

★ Fifth Avenue, with its _____ department stores, is the most famous shopping street in New York. But be sure to check out Canal Street and Chinatown, too. Locals appreciate these areas for their interesting smaller shops.

★ There are many _____ _____ in busy shopping _____. Some will tell you they're selling real brand-name clothes, shoes, and accessories, but the items may not be _____. If the price seems too good to be true, you should probably _____ the item in a store instead.

B Create a Poster

In a small group, create a similar poster about your city (or another city you all know well). Include tips about getting around, safety, shopping, and any other important information for visitors. Present your poster to the class.

C Reminder

Some Module 4 Goals in Unit 8

Put a check mark (✓) next to the things you can do.

_____ Understand instructions expressed in simple language (for example, how to use public telephones or ticket machines, safety information, or directions)

_____ Write a short, formal email asking for or giving simple information

_____ Write simple texts about experiences or events (for example, describing your feelings and reactions about a trip)

Warm Up

With a partner, put the words and phrases from the box into the correct categories. Some words can be put in more than one category.

| turn on | transfer | character | rush hour | receipt |
| log in | device | cash | exchange | commuter |

Transportation	Shopping	Electronics/Games

Brainstorm

You and your partner have just arrived at your favorite shopping mall. Discuss ideas for spending the day there. Consider what you will do, what you'd like to buy or need to buy, where you will eat, and how you will fill the day. You need to stay at the mall from the morning to the evening.

Role-play

Now, using your ideas from part B, create a detailed plan for the day with your partner and write a conversation. Perform your conversation for the class.

Plan

1. _____
2. _____
3. _____
4. _____

Conversation

A: _____
B: _____
A: _____
B: _____
A: _____
B: _____
A: _____
B: _____

Module 4 Review

A Vocabulary

Write the words, and choose the correct answers to complete the sentences.

1. Write four words related to restaurants.

   _____ _____ _____ _____

2. Write five phrasal verbs from the module.

   _____ _____ _____ _____ _____

3. It isn't a _____ flight—there's a short _____ in Mexico City. But the _____ is cheap.
   a. connection, layover, economy class
   b. direct, layover, airfare
   c. non-stop, round-trip, connection

4. I booked a(n) _____ motel, so there's no _____ or other _____.
   a. inexpensive, room service, amenities
   b. comfortable, suite, amenities
   c. overnight, room service, décor

5. This store has a great _____ of clothes, but it's not _____ to drive to, especially during _____.
   a. selection, terrific, showings   b. level, convenient, purchase   c. selection, convenient, rush hour

6. As long as you have your _____, you can return an item for _____ or for _____.
   a. receipt, cash, store credit   b. belongings, exchange, cash   c. store credit, duty-free, trade in

7. The North Hills _____ thanks you for your business, and we _____ you to stop by our food court to try some delicious _____!
   a. Motel, appreciate, room service   b. Mall, encourage, cuisines   c. Mall, proceed, souvenirs

B Grammar

Look back at the module. Fill in the blanks.

1. When I was young, we _____ always stay in motels on family trips.

2. She's a student with a job, so she's used _____ working hard.

3. How long _____ you been living there?

4. _____ we book the tickets now, we won't get good seats.

5. _____ the exams weren't next week, we could stay on vacation longer.

6. Don't buy the first laptop you see. You should shop _____ first.

7. Her hair _____ to be blonde, but then she dyed it red.

8. If we _____ a fitness tracker, we _____ know the distance.

9. We need to make a reservation a few days in advance. _____, we won't get a table.

10. He has _____ waiting for over an hour!

11. When I woke up, Mom _____ already cooked breakfast.

12. You seem stressed. If I were you, I _____ take a vacation.

13. It's cold! Put your hat and gloves _____.

14. At first it was hard to exercise every day, but I got _____ to it.

15. Did you _____ that Beth got a new boyfriend?

16. To _____ the characters _____ move, press here.

C Best Way to Travel?

Imagine you are planning a long-distance trip. Would you rather drive, take a train, or fly? Why? Discuss your reasons with a partner.

D How to Play

Think of a game that you know (a video game or board game). Describe it to a partner, including how to play it. Your partner should take notes to help him or her remember.

> Notes
>
>

What does your partner think of the game? Does he or she want to play it? Why or why not? Tell the class.

E Dream Trip

1. Imagine that you are planning a surprise trip for a married couple you're close to for their wedding anniversary. You and a partner are both friends of the couple. First, look at the images below and choose which destination you would like to send the couple to.

Italy

Morocco

Austria

2. Either you or your partner would make the travel arrangements and plan two activities in the destination. The other person would make the accommodation arrangements as well as the restaurant bookings. Working separately, write a detailed summary of your plan for the couple.

_____

_____

_____

_____

_____

_____

3. Then, together, create a detailed itinerary of the trip that you can present to the couple as a surprise. Present it to the class as though you were presenting it to the couple as their anniversary gift.

I'm staying in tonight.

Lesson 1 **Present continuous with present and future reference**

We use the present continuous to show something that is happening now or that will happen in the future.

You are reading. → Are you reading?

present continuous: subject + be + verb-ing		
statement	**negative**	**question**
They **are sleeping**.	They **are not / aren't sleeping**.	**Are** they **sleeping**?
about the present		**about the future**
The present continuous is usually about actions happening right now. Time expressions such as (*right*) *now* or *currently* can be used.		The present continuous can also be used for definite future plans. Future time expressions such as *tomorrow* can be used.
I'm eating breakfast (now). They **are shopping** (currently).		**I'm going** to work (tomorrow). My friend **is visiting** me (soon).

Lesson 2 **Simple present vs. present continuous**

We use the simple present for routine actions and general facts. We use the present continuous for actions that are happening now, temporary facts, and future plans.

I wear glasses.   *I'm wearing my glasses right now.*

simple present vs. present continuous			
simple present		**present continuous**	
routine actions	She **shops** every day. I **do** yoga on Sundays.	actions now	She **is shopping** now. **I'm doing** yoga right now.
general facts	The artist **paints** beautifully. He **works** nearby.	temporary facts	He **is working** nearby for a few weeks.
		future plans	**I'm babysitting** tomorrow.

Lesson 3 **Action verbs and stative verbs**

Action verbs describe the act of doing something. Stative verbs are verbs of states or feelings.

She is running. (action)   *She seems tired.* (stative)

action verbs
Many verbs are action verbs. These are verbs that describe someone or something doing an action, moving, or changing. Examples include *eat*, *play*, and *watch*. These verbs can be used in present continuous sentences: *She is eating soup.*
stative verbs
Stative verbs do not describe an action, movement, or change. Examples include *be, remember, understand, love,* and *hate*. These verbs are not usually used in the present continuous. They are often used in the simple present: *This soup is cold. I hate it!*

verbs with both uses
Some verbs can be both action verbs and stative verbs. For example, *have* is stative when it means to own: *He has an umbrella.* But *have* can also mean experience or to eat. Then it's an action verb and can be used in the present continuous: *He's having fun.* *We're having breakfast.*

Lesson 4 **Expressing preferences with *would rather***

We use *would rather* to express what we prefer more than something else.

I would rather eat pasta than have pizza.

would rather + verb phrase + than + verb phrase
Compare two actions with *would rather... than*: *I **would rather** play basketball **than** watch it on TV.* This means you would like the first action more than the second. In questions, you can use *or* to compare two options: ***Would** he **rather** go out **or** stay home?*
simpler forms
If we already know what is being compared, we don't need the *than* clause. Just use *would rather*: *She doesn't want to watch a reality show. She **would rather** watch a sitcom.* The short form of *would* is often used: *I'**d rather** play basketball.* *She'**d rather** watch a sitcom.*

Lesson 5 **Expressing preferences and making comparisons with *prefer* and *as... as***

We use *prefer* to show our preference for something over another thing.

I prefer dogs to cats.
I prefer to play with kids rather than work with adults.

prefer + noun + to + noun	prefer to + verb (+ rather than + verb)
Compare two nouns or gerunds with *prefer... to*: *She **prefers** apples **to** oranges.* *He **prefers** going out **to** staying in.*	*Prefer* can also be followed by an infinitive: *I don't like to wear glasses.* *I **prefer to** use contact lenses.* Use *prefer to* and *rather than* to compare two verb phrases: *I **prefer to** ride a bike **rather than** lift weights.*
would prefer	
Use *would prefer* when talking about a choice you're making now. *A: Would you like an appetizer?* *B: Thanks, but I **would (I'd) prefer** to just have the main meal.*	
not as + adjective + as	
The phrase *not as* + adjective + *as* means *less* + adjective + *than*. *The bus is **not as fast as** the train.* = *The bus is slower than the train. The train is faster than the bus.*	

Unit 2
I'll go out tonight.

Lesson 1 Future tense

We can use *will* and *be going to* to talk about the future. Often, both *will* and *be going to* can be used.

I will watch a movie. = I am going to watch a movie.

future tense with *will* and *be going to*	
We can speak about the future using *will* or *be going to*. Often, you can use either *will* or *be going to*: *I will see you later.* *I am going to see you later.*	
will	**be going to**
With *if* (first conditional): *If you study, you will get a good grade.*	For decisions and definite plans made before speaking: *I cooked dinner for my family. We are going to eat now.*
For offers to do something: *The phone's ringing. I'll get it.*	

Lesson 2 Making predictions and expressing probability with *will* and *be going to*

making predictions			
You can make a prediction (give an opinion about the future) using either *will* or *be going to*. *It'll snow tomorrow. = It's going to snow tomorrow.*			
expressing probability			
maybe	possibly	perhaps	probably
Maybe is often used as a sentence adverb. It means that something is possible but not certain.	*Possibly* can be used after *will*, or *be* verbs and as a sentence adverb. It's not often spoken.	*Perhaps* is like *maybe*, but it is used more often in writing than in conversation.	*Probably* is stronger than *maybe*, *possibly*, or *perhaps*. It means you are almost sure.
Maybe we are going to play against the red team.	My boss will **possibly** meet you next week.	**Perhaps** we aren't going to finish our project tonight.	I'll **probably** fail the exam.

Lesson 3 Modals of possibility

A modal adds meaning to the main verb. Modals of possibility say how sure you are about something.

She should graduate this year. She may then get married.

modals of possibility		
meaning	**modals**	**examples**
possibility	*could, may, might*	These flowers **could** be a present for me! My boyfriend **may** meet us later. This restaurant **might** serve vegetarian food.
strong possibility	*should, ought to*	This paint **ought to** look great for the fence. She left fifteen minutes ago. She **should** get here soon.
near certainty	*must, can't*	If you like pasta, you **must** love this great Italian restaurant. He **can't / must not** be your twin. You don't look anything alike!

Lesson 4 *That* clauses

That clauses are often used with verbs about thoughts, ideas, speech, and advice. *That* clauses can also be used after many adjectives for thoughts, feelings, and possibility.

After a verb: *I bet **that** you are a student.*

After an adjective: *I am hopeful **that** he will tell the truth.*

that clauses					
verbs and adjectives which take *that* clauses					
verbs			adjectives		
think	guess	say	certain	aware	likely
believe	know	agree	sure	worried	possible
hope	bet	promise	convinced	hopeful	impossible
expect	decide	understand	important	afraid	sorry
forget	feel	imagine	sure	pleased	surprised

Lesson 5 Suggesting activities

We can suggest activities using a variety of sentence starters, including *let's, suggest*, modal verbs, and questions.

Let's *eat dinner now.*

let's	suggest (that)
The most common way to propose something is with *let's* + verb: **Let's** dance!	Use *suggest + that* clause: I **suggest** that we take the train there.
modal verbs	**questions as suggestions**
Could, should, and *ought to* are often used for suggestions: We **could** order takeout. You **ought to** go to their concert. He **should** join a gym.	*Why not* + verb: **Why not** come to the party? *What about* + gerund: **What about** going for a bike ride? *Why don't you* + verb: **Why don't you** join us?

Lesson 1 Gerunds and infinitives

A gerund is an *-ing* verb used as a noun. An infinitive is *to* + verb.

*She enjoys **dancing**.*   *We agreed **to meet**.*

gerunds (verb-*ing*)	infinitives (*to* + verb)
As the subject of a sentence or after the *be* verb: ***Skiing** is my favorite sport.* *My favorite sport is **skiing**.*	After certain verbs (for example, *like, choose, agree, want*): *We **agreed to clean** our rooms on Sunday.*
After a preposition: *He is good **at singing** in class.*	After some adjectives (for example, *fun, able, nice*): *The books are **fun to read**.*
After certain verbs (for example, *like, enjoy, mind, practice*): *I **practice speaking** English.*	After *know how*: *I **know how to play** baseball.*
After *go* (for example, *shopping, dancing,* and some other activities): *Let's **go hiking/dancing**.*	

Lesson 2 Suggestions and advice with gerunds, infinitives, modals, and *that* clauses

We use gerunds, infinitives, modals, and *that* clauses to give advice or make suggestions.

I suggest eating at the restaurant.

suggestions and advice with gerunds and infinitives	
I suggest / I recommend + gerund	
*I **recommend watching** the game.* *I **suggest going** on Monday.* Using *I suggest / recommend* + gerund sounds more formal than using infinitives or modal verbs.	
be sure / it's a good idea + infinitive	
Be sure to go to the basketball game. **It's a good idea to arrive** early.	

strong advice with the modal *had better*	suggestions with *that* clauses
subject + (*had*) *better* + verb	*I suggest / recommend* + *that* clause
We**'d better not be** late. = We **better not be** late.	*I **recommend (that)** they go cheer at the game.* = *I **suggest (that)** they go cheer at the game.*

Lesson 3 Future continuous tense

We use the future continuous for future actions that continue for a period of time.

I will be traveling for a week.

future continuous tense
You can use the future continuous to talk about future actions that continue for a period of time. It is formed with *will / be going to* + *be* + verb-*ing*.

a future action lasting for a while	
with *will*	with *be going to*
He**'ll be working** in America for three months. She **won't be exercising** Monday evening. **Will** you **be traveling** on the weekend?	I**'m going to be lifting** weights this afternoon. They**'re not going to be eating** out for some time. **Are** you **going to be doing** yoga tonight?

a future action happening at a specific time
Meet me after class. I**'ll be waiting** in my car.

Lesson 4 Empty *it* and *that* clauses

We use empty *it* with *that* clauses to talk about suggestions, rules, recommendations, and opinions.

It is required that you sleep eight hours a night during the competition.

It is + adjective + *that* clause
It is + adjective + *that* clause can be used with certain adjectives to talk about suggestions, rules, and recommendations. These adjectives include *recommended, important, necessary,* and *required*.
Exercising with a personal trainer is recommended. = **It is recommended that** you exercise with a personal trainer. Eating a healthy diet is important. = **It's important that** you eat a healthy diet.
You can also use *it is* + adjective + *that* clause with some other adjectives about opinions. These include *good, great, amazing, terrible,* and *possible*.
It's great that you're going on vacation.

Lesson 5 Intensifiers

We use intensifiers to make the meaning of adjectives stronger.

*The sun is **extremely** hot.*

intensifiers	
Use intensifiers to make the meaning of adjectives stronger. The intensifier can be a word or a phrase. It comes before the adjective: *You are **so** clever!*	
common intensifiers	
a bit / a little so / really / very / super	pretty / fairly / quite extremely
comparing using intensifiers	
Some intensifiers (*even, so much, a lot*) can be used with comparative adjectives. Other intensifiers cannot.	
My stomach feels **a lot better** now. It's **even colder** today than yesterday. He's **so much bigger** than his brother.	

Lesson 1 Present perfect tense

We use the present perfect to talk about past events that have a connection to the present.

I've had trouble breathing since yesterday.

present perfect: *have/has* + past participle		
meaning	**common expressions**	**examples**
past state/action that continues to the present	*for* + period of time *since* + point in time	I've **had** the flu since last week. She's **lived** here since 2015.
experience	*before, ever, never, once, twice, ~ times*	A: **Have** you (ever) **been** to Australia before? B: No, I **haven't**. / Yes, I've **been** there once.
change over time	*since* + point in time	She's **grown** so much since last month.
completed actions	*already, yet*	I've already **completed** my homework. **Have** you **finished** it yet?
recent events with an effect on the present; news	*just*	He's **eaten** some bad food. I've just **seen** a doctor.

Note For regular verbs, the past participle is the same as the simple past form. Some verbs are irregular.

Lesson 2 Present perfect vs. simple past

We use the present perfect for past actions that are still not finished and the simple past for past actions that are finished.

I've had headaches for years.
She had a headache last night.

present perfect vs. simple past	
present perfect	Use the present perfect to talk about an action or state that is not finished. It has a connection to the present.
	I've **lived** here for seven years. (I still live here.)
	Use the present perfect when the time of a past action is not important or not known.
	I **haven't had** an illness for a long time.
simple past	Use the simple past to talk about an action or state that happened in the past and is finished.
	I **worked** in Japan until 2014.
	Use the simple past with past time expressions.
	She **had** pizza **last night**.

Lesson 3 *too* and *enough*; *want / would like* + object + infinitive

We use *too/enough* to say something about amounts or degrees.

We use *want / would like* to talk about wants.

There's been too much rain lately.
He would like to have dinner.

too and enough	
too	**enough**
Too is an adverb meaning "more than what is needed or wanted." It comes before an adjective or adverb.	*Enough* is an adverb meaning "equal to what is needed; to the necessary degree." It comes after an adjective or adverb.
He's **too** lazy to brush his teeth.	I was not fast **enough** to win.

want / would like + object + infinitive	
You use the structure *want / would like* + object + infinitive to talk about something you want someone to do.	
I **want my mother to get** an X-ray.	

Lesson 4 Past continuous tense; *when* clauses

We use the past continuous for actions that continued for some time in the past.

They were leaving the house.
They were leaving when I showed up.

past continuous: *was/were* + verb-*ing*
a past ongoing action
She **was spending** a lot of time at the gym. He **wasn't eating** much last week.
a past action that was ongoing at a specific time
They **were meditating** at 10:30 last night.
questions and negatives
A: **Were** you **taking** a break? B: Yes, I **was**. / No, I **wasn't**. I **wasn't taking** a break. Q: **What was** he **doing**?   A: He **was eating**.
***when* clauses**
Use *when* clauses with the past continuous to talk about something that interrupted or happened during a continuous action. Use the simple past in the *when* clause.
You were bathing from 6:00 to 7:00. They arrived at 6:30. → You **were bathing when** they arrived. She was cooking from 12:00 to 1:00. I left at 12:30. → She **was cooking when** I left.

Lesson 5 Modals of obligation

Modals of obligation are used to talk about something that is necessary.

She must see the doctor every six months.

modals of obligation: modal + base verb		
weak obligation: advice, suggestions, warnings		
should (not)	ought to	had better (not)
A: **Should** I start treatment right away? B: Yes, you **should** start treatment right away. You **shouldn't** wait.	I **ought to** see a doctor about my illness. You **ought to** take your car in for a checkup soon.	She'**d better** go to the pharmacy before it closes. She'**d better not** wait.
strong obligation: necessity		
must (not)	(not) have to	had got to
You **must** remember to floss every day. You **must not** / **shouldn't** forget.	A: **Do I have to** take allergy pills every day? B: No, you **don't have to** take them every day. But you **must** take them as directed.	You **have got to** get a prescription. You'**ve got to** see a doctor.

Lesson 1 Reported speech with infinitives; *about* for topic

We use *said* or *told* and the infinitive of a verb to report someone's instructions, advice, or suggestions.

"You need to get more exercise," he said. → He told me to get more exercise. / He said to get more exercise.

reported speech with infinitives
said + (*not*) infinitive / *told* + object + (*not*) infinitive

"You need to get more sleep," the doctor said. →	The doctor **said to get** more sleep.
"Have another cookie," Victor said (to me). →	Victor **told me to have** another cookie.
"Don't use heavy weights," Gloria said (to her). →	Gloria **told her not to use** heavy weights.

reported speech with *about* for topic
talked about / *told* + object + *about*

"On our second date, we went for dinner, and then…" →	He **told me about** their second date.
"I've eaten at many restaurants. I like…" →	She **talked about** restaurants she has visited.

Lesson 2 Zero conditional

We use zero conditional sentences to talk about general facts in the present. Both clauses in the sentence use the simple present.

If you exercise a lot, then your body burns more calories.

zero conditional		
	condition	result
If	you **exercise,** you**'re** old,	(then) you **have** more energy. (then) your body **slows** down.
	they **have** a big lunch,	(then) they don't **feel** hungry in the afternoon.

Lesson 3 Reported speech with *that* clauses

To report past statements that are still true, use a past tense reporting verb (for example, *said*) with a simple present verb in the reported speech.

"I like fruit," he said. → He said that he likes fruit.

reported speech with *that* clauses
subject + *said* (*that*) + clause subject + *told* + object + (*that*) + clause

"Vegetables are so bland," he said. → He **said** (**that**) vegetables are bland.
"You shouldn't eat before lunch," my dad said (to me). → My dad **told me** (**that**) I shouldn't eat before lunch.

Lesson 4 Reported speech with simple present tense

We use a reporting verb in the simple present to talk about things that people say often, opinions that people still hold, and things that are written on signs, labels, etc.

"Salad is good for lunch," my doctor tells me. → My doctor tells me that salad is good for lunch.

reported speech with the simple present
subject + *say(s)* (*that*) + clause subject + *tell(s)* + object + (*that*) + clause

"Fruit is good for breakfast," she says (to me). → She **tells me** (**that**) fruit is good for breakfast.
"You must read the food label," Penny always says. → Penny always **says** (**that**) we must read the food label.
Protein   0% → The label **says** (**that**) there's no protein.

Lesson 5 First conditional

We use first conditional sentences to make *if* statements about the future.

The *if* clause is in the simple present, and the result clause is in the future tense.

If you eat a lot of beans, then you will get enough protein.

first conditional		
	condition	result
If	you **don't eat** enough vegetables,	(then) you **will get** sick easily.
	you **cook** the meat too long,	(then) it **will burn**.
	we **eat** a lot of oranges, he **keeps** eating fast food,	(then) we**'ll get** enough vitamin C. (then) he **won't be** healthy.

Lesson 1 Tag questions

We use tag questions when we expect a certain response.

A: You were bathing, weren't you?
B: Yes, I was.

tag questions		
Tag questions are added at the end of statements. They are used when the speaker expects a certain answer and just wants to make sure. Positive statements are followed by negative tag questions, and negative statements are followed by positive tag questions. The form of a tag question is auxiliary verb (+ *not*) + subject? (Auxiliary verbs include *be, do, have,* and modals.) Contractions are almost always used.		
positive statement	**negative tag question**	**expected answer**
We **need** to buy soap,	**don't** we?	Yes, we do.
That's a new shirt,	**isn't** it?	Yes, it is.
I **took** your towel,	**didn't** I?	Yes, you did.
negative statement	**positive tag question**	**expected answer**
He **never brushes** his hair,	**does** he?	No, he doesn't.
You **won't be** early,	**will** you?	No, I won't.
You **haven't showered,**	**have** you?	No, I haven't.

Lesson 2 Negative questions

We use negative questions when we expect the answer to be yes or to express surprise at unexpected news and to ask about it.

The negative form of the question word is used.

A: I'd better be going.
B: Now? Aren't you staying for dinner?

negative questions	
negative question	**expected answer**
Don't you use sunscreen?	Yes, I do.
Shouldn't he use moisturizer?	Yes, he should.
Isn't this good for dry skin?	Yes, it is.
Wouldn't you like some lotion?	Yes, I would.

Lesson 3 Content clauses with *if* and *whether*

We can create statements with *if/whether* content clauses from yes/no questions.

Did he shave his head? → She wants to know if he shaved his head.

content clauses with *if* and *whether*	
Yes/no questions can be made into content clauses beginning with *if* or *whether.* They have the form *if/whether* + subject + verb phrase. These clauses often follow verbs such as *know, remember, decide, ask, check,* etc. These clauses may or may not end with *or not.* Questions giving two choices (with *or*) can also be made into *if/whether* content clauses. These clauses do not end with *or not.*	
direct question	**statement with content clause**
Does she have bangs?	We can't remember **if/whether** she has bangs (or not).
Did he dye his hair?	Ask him **if/whether** he dyed his hair (or not).
Is that his sister or his cousin?	I don't know **if/whether** that is his sister or his cousin.

Lesson 4 Content clauses with *wh-* questions

We can also use *wh-* questions to make content clauses.

Where did you get your haircut? → He asked where I got my haircut.

content clauses with *wh-* questions	
Like yes/no questions, *wh-* questions can become content clauses. These content clauses take this form: *wh-* word/phrase + subject + verb phrase. They follow many of the same verbs as *if/whether* clauses.	
***wh-* question**	**statement with content clause**
What hairstyle would you like?	He wants to know **what hairstyle** she would like.
When can I get my manicure?	The customer is asking **when** she can get her manicure.

Lesson 5 Passive voice

We use the passive voice when the doer of the action is unknown or not important.

The stylist cut my bangs. → My bangs were cut by the stylist.

passive voice	

Most sentences are in the active voice. This means the subject is the doer of the action:
    The spa offers massages.
 	
 When the doer of an action is unknown or is less important, we use the passive voice. In the passive voice, the subject receives the action:
    *Massages **are offered** (by the spa).*
 	
 The form of the passive is *be* + past participle. The verb *be* shows the tense.	

active	**passive**
We **give** a 25% discount.	A 25% discount **is given** (by us).
Our staff **will take care of** you.	You **will be taken care of** (by our staff).

Lesson 1 Second conditional

Second conditional sentences use an *if* clause and a *would* clause to talk about something that is not true in the present or something that probably won't happen in the future.

If I were self-employed, I would have more time to travel.

second conditional	
if clause: condition	*would* clause: result
If he **didn't like** Ecuador,	(then) he **wouldn't visit** every year. (He does like Ecuador.)
If he **didn't work** on weekends,	he **would go** camping. (He does work on the weekends.)
If I **lost** my passport,	I **wouldn't be** able to go home. (I didn't lose my passport.)
The *would* clause can come first. No comma is needed in this case. *My parents **would be** mad if I got into a fight at school.*	

Lesson 2 *would* and *used to*

Both *would* + verb and *used to* + verb can be used to talk about habits or things that happened repeatedly in the past but do not happen now.

I would drink coffee every day in university.

	would + verb	*used to* + verb
statement	We **would go** to England every summer.	I **used to play** tennis with my cousin.
negative	I **wouldn't want** to go home after visiting my grandmother.	She **didn't use to want** to travel on her own.
question	**Would** you **miss** your friends while living abroad?	**Did** your mother **use to worry** about you?

Lesson 3 *be used to* and *get used to*

Be used to describes what somebody is already familiar with and comfortable doing. *Get used to* describes what somebody is becoming familiar with and comfortable doing.

I'm used to waking up at 6:00.
I'm getting used to the weather here.

be used to + noun/gerund	*get used to* + noun/gerund
I'm **used to driving** everywhere. He **is used to living** alone. She **isn't used to** spicy **food**. **Is** Alex **used to staying** up late?	I **got used to eating** rice every day. Lisa **is getting used to** her new **computer**. He **will get used to** his new **job**.

Lesson 4 Reported speech with *I heard*

We use *I heard* to talk about information that is less certain or trustworthy.

I heard that Barbados is really beautiful.

Reported speech with *I heard*
Dan **heard that** she's quitting her job.
She **heard** tickets to Australia are cheap these days.
They **heard that** you moved back home.
Did you **hear that** his father is in the hospital?

Lesson 5 Past perfect tense

We use the past perfect to talk about something that happened before something else in the past.

By the time dinner was ready, I had finished my homework.

past perfect	
the action happened before a specific past time (often with *at/by* + time)	She didn't come home. It was 11 o'clock (then). → She **hadn't come** home by 11 o'clock.
	John left before 5 o'clock. → At 5 o'clock, John **had** (already) **left**.
the action happened before a specific past event (often with a simple past clause using *by the time* or *when*)	My cell phone died. Then you tried to call me. → By the time you tried to call me, my cell phone **had died**.
	She was at the party an hour. Then I arrived. → She **had** (already) **been** at the party for an hour when I arrived.

Lesson 1 Phrasal verbs

Phrasal verbs consist of a verb and another element, such as an adverb (*break down*) or preposition (*talk about*). They are usually used in informal situations. There are two types: inseparable and separable.

It's best to shop around for a car.
I have to look her phone number up.

phrasal verbs		
	examples	sentences
inseparable	*hang out, drop by, get around, shop around (for), miss out (on), log in/out, sign in/out*	I **dropped by** the bookstore on my way home. Louis **gets around** the city by bus.
separable	*turn on/off, pick up, think over, throw away, look up, find out, check out, put on, take off, drop off*	I will **pick up** some flowers later. I'll **pick them up** after work.

Lesson 2 Ways to express conditions

Besides the word *if*, there are several ways to talk about conditions in English.

ways to express conditions		
expression	meaning	example
as long as / so long as (conjunctions)	(only) if	You can go out tonight **as long as** you don't have any homework. **So long as** we have a map, we shouldn't get lost.
unless (conjunction)	If not... then	**Unless** I go with her, she will spend all her money.
otherwise (sentence adverb)	if not	I have to leave now. **Otherwise**, I won't be able to catch the bus.

Lesson 3 Present perfect continuous tense

We use the present perfect continuous to describe something that started in the past but may still be happening or has just finished.

I've been looking to buy a new phone the last couple months.

present perfect continuous	
have/has + *been* + present participle	
the action has been ongoing and is not finished	I've **been trying** to call him all day. (I still am.) Alicia **hasn't been saving** up money. (She still isn't.) What **have** you **been studying** in school? (You still are.)
the action has been ongoing and has recently finished	It's nice to eat something different. I've **been eating** a lot of rice recently. You were very quiet the last few days. **Have** you **been feeling** unwell?

Lesson 4 Causative verbs

The verbs *make*, *get*, and *have* can be used to talk about causing someone to do something or causing something to happen.

My sister made me go shopping with her.
I got the waiter to bring me another drink.

causative verbs	
make/have + object + base verb	My mom **made me do** my homework before I could play computer games. (I didn't want to do my homework first.) **I'll have my friend send** me more information. (I'll ask her.)
get + object + infinitive	I **can't get the dog to stop** barking.

Lesson 5 Leaving out articles for brevity

Sometimes, there is a need to leave out articles (*a, an, the*) to make sentences short and easy to read on posters and signs as well as in newspaper headlines.

leaving out articles for brevity
Caution: Stand clear of the door → Caution: Stand clear of door A dog saves a man from drowning. → Dog Saves Man from Drowning

Unit 1
I'm staying in tonight.

Lesson 1
band
club
football
grilled salmon
jazz
plans
get-together
invite
join in
stay in

Lesson 2
turkey
vegetable
prepare
wait
delicious
favorite
starving
tasty
dig in
help yourself
set the table
take out

Lesson 3
minute
point
teammate
explain
guess
remember
think
understand
complicated
simple

Lesson 4
channel
nature show
news
reality show
remote
sitcom
soap opera
on

Lesson 5
comedy
comic book
fiction
non-fiction
novel

performance
review
screen
be about

Unit 2
I'll go out tonight.

Lesson 1
grandchild
grandchildren
nephew
niece
Thanksgiving
miss
mother-in-law
be on (one's) way
look forward to
run late

Lesson 2
double date
hobby
cancel
worry
perfect
shy
be stressed out
be yourself
get to know (someone)
go on a blind date
It's no big deal.

Lesson 3
action movie
fantasy
horror movie
romantic comedy
animated
hilarious
scary
sold out
violent

Lesson 4
bar
bartender
concert
cover charge
live music
agree
believe
bet
dance
hope
know
promise

say
aware
certain
convinced
hopeful
impossible
likely
possible
sure
worried
feel like

Lesson 5
coast
day trip
downtown
music festival
relieve
outdoors
It's been a long week.

Unit 3
Sports and Fitness

Lesson 1
athlete
diving
event
figure skating
gymnastics
move
skiing
surfing
the Olympics
compete
dream
graceful
terrible

Lesson 2
basketball
second
score
excellent
left
behind
on
show up

Lesson 3
energy
fitness
membership
workout
join
strong
get in shape

lift weights
lose weight
work out

Lesson 4
exercise equipment
muscle
nutrition
personal trainer
protein
treadmill
free
healthy
important
necessary
get hurt

Lesson 5
ankle
bandage
calf
cheek
chin
earlobe
elbow
eyebrow
forehead
ice
injury
knee
neck
pain reliever
shoulder
stomach
thigh
wrist
put
painful
serious
What's the matter?

Unit 4
Take care of yourself.

Lesson 1
cancellation
flu
headache
illness
medication/medicine
patient
symptom
vomit
nasty
similar
trouble breathing

Lesson 2

allergy
body aches
congestion
cough
cure
fever
food poisoning
nausea
pill
prescription
runny nose
sore throat
gone
I can't keep anything
down.

Lesson 3

cavity
dentist
filling
gums
hygienist
mouthwash
physician
staining
teeth
X-ray
bleed
floss
rinse
common
too bad

Lesson 4

blog
relationship
therapist
counsel
meditate
emotional
mental
physical
social
regularly

Lesson 5

capsule
chest
dose
label
pharmacist
side effects
treatment
cause
effective
at a time

Unit 5
Eat Right

Lesson 1

checkup
clinic
diet
fat
lungs
olive oil
heal
sugary
alcoholic
according to
cut down on

Lesson 2

bone
calorie
calcium
nutrient
pound
protein
sex
vitamin
burn
average

Lesson 3

beans
cancer
disease
recipe
risk
spice
steak
vegetarian
bland

Lesson 4

blender
fridge
ingredient
serving
smoothie
wheat
yogurt
frozen
nutritious

Lesson 5

broccoli
cup
directions
method
pepper
saucepan

tablespoon
chop
combine
reduce
remove
stir-fry

Unit 6
Look Good, Feel Good

Lesson 1

argument
cream
mirror
suit
comb
shampoo
shave
patient
put on

Lesson 2

acne
brand
cleanser
lotion
makeup
moisturizer
product
skin
soap
sunscreen
sweat
gentle
oily

Lesson 3

bangs
barber
dyed hair
hairstylist/hairdresser
perm
ponytail
salon
bald
shoulder-length
spiky
stand out from the crowd

Lesson 4

clippers
fingernail
grooming
hygiene
infection
manicure
nail file

nail polish
pedicure
toenail
affect

Lesson 5

accommodations
coconut
discount
massage
spa
bathe
cover
disappear
pamper
scrub
luxurious
soothing

Unit 7
Planning Ahead

Lesson 1

airfare
connection
destination
economy class
layover
direct
non-stop
round-trip
depart

Lesson 2

air-conditioning
amenities
double room
room service
suite
vacation
comfortable
inexpensive
overnight
check out

Lesson 3

key
lend
rent
share
unlock
convenient
plus
be worth it
by the (hour, day, etc.)
get around
in advance

Lesson 4

chef
decor
patio
server
celebrate
rave
gorgeous
terrific

Lesson 5

box office
mall
showing
hurry
embarrassed
exactly
smoothly
cheer up

Lesson 4

cash
character
level
point of view
space
store credit
trade-in
weapon
customize
pre-order

Lesson 5

belongings
emergency
exchange
receipt
valuables
collect
proceed
aware
cautious
duty-free

Unit 8
Shopping Trips

Lesson 1

accessory
cuisine
district
electronics
selection
souvenir
street vendor
fashionable
genuine
imported
get tired of

Lesson 2

commuter
fare
line
rush hour
calculate
transfer
stuck
depend on

Lesson 3

device
fitness tracker
purchase
appreciate
encourage
remind
enormous
keep an eye on
run out of